TRAVELLERS IN THE SAND

Desert lands of the Near East, a journal of true adventure

Travellers in the Sand

Published by The Conrad Press in the United Kingdom 2021

Tel: +44(0)1227 472 874
www.theconradpress.com
info@theconradpress.com

ISBN 978-1-914913-30-3

Typesetting and Cover Design by: Charlotte Mouncey, www.bookstyle.co.uk
Cover image created with authors own images

The Conrad Press logo was designed by Maria Priestley.

Printed and bound in Great Britain by Clays Ltd, Elcograf S.p.A.

ALSO BY JIM TAYLOR:

Wheels of Steel –
a rollercoaster ride of adventures by road and by rail

Published by The Conrad Press (2019)
ISBN 978-1-911546-60-3
£9.99 Also available as an ebook

Hot Metal –
a motorcycle adventure ride like no other

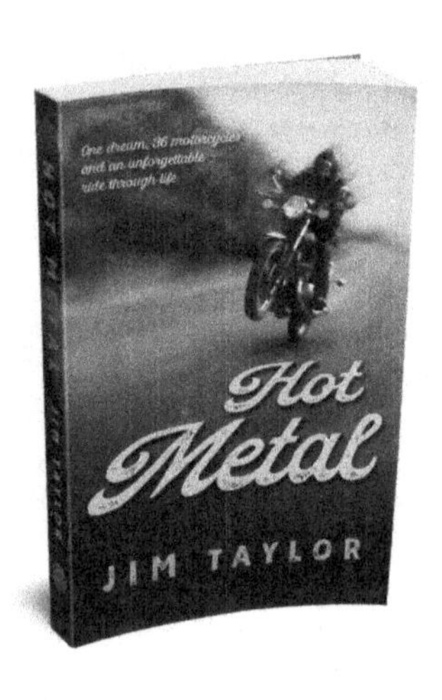

Published by The Conrad Press (2020)
ISBN 978-1-913567-05-7
£9.99 Also available as an ebook

TRAVELLERS IN THE SAND

Desert lands of the Near East,
a journal of true adventure

JIM TAYLOR

I've been through the desert on a horse with no name
It felt good to be out of the rain
In the desert you can remember your name
'Cause there ain't no one for to give you no pain
La, la …

written by Dewey Bunnell,
and originally recorded by the folk rock band America.

INTRODUCTION

The definition of an 'adventure', I once heard, is: a risky venture with an unknown outcome. I like to remind myself of that definition whenever the phrase 'adventure travel' is banded about.

I was born in a gamekeeper's cottage on the Berkshire Downs in mid-winter and was four years old when my family moved to rural Kent. I spent a hard childhood growing up on a rundown smallholding, on which we struggled to make a subsistence living, doing things the right way. I loved the old-fashioned pioneering spirit it evoked, recycling stuff and making do.

We were as self-sufficient as it was possible to be, but it couldn't be sustained on the small amount of land we farmed. Then, when we managed to get hold of more land, we found we didn't have enough people in the family to work it. We never had a family holiday; not one, and I knew I would have to get out there and discover the world for myself just as soon as I was able.

I was a dreamer and my school days were largely huge chunks of wasted time, but I do remember one detention I sat, where a group of us young thugs were told to list our ambitions and think about how we were going to achieve them. I was still writing when the others were leaving the classroom after being excused. I'd got more out of that detention session than the teacher imagined. The one thing I do remember writing down was a plan to cross the Sahara in a big truck and mental images of that dream never really stopped inspiring me to plan that next risky venture with an uncertain outcome.

Jim Taylor October 2021

CONTENTS

PREFACE

From as long as I can remember, fuelled by images implanted in my mind when I was a child, I have yearned to experience the desert, in all its majesty and desolation. It is the heat, the sand, the colour and texture of baked and scoured rock – as well as the enormous and perfect night sky. It is a landscape as old as time itself and maybe the last one that man can ruin.

But there is life there still, in a fashion which is connected to and characteristic of biblical times. It is rare now, in the second decade of the twenty first century, to have the privilege of viewing life as a normal state – unchanged in almost every way; family life and people following the cycles of nature and the instincts of survival in a harsh environment, where water is the precious element enabling a subsistence culture to survive.

Well let me tell you another story…

If you remember tales from *The Arabian Nights, Ali Baba and the Forty Thieves, The Thief of Bagdad, Sinbad the Sailor* – or even the images from the *Fry's Turkish Delight* advert – then you will know how the Middle East was portrayed to children when I was at primary school. I remember laughing so much at that Laurel and Hardy short film, where they went to join the French Foreign Legion in North Africa and successfully defended their fort from hordes of attacking Arabs in baggy robes and bare feet: by scattering out barrel loads of tin tacks across the ground within the walls, and then they just opened up the doors.

There were the old films they used to put on weekend TV in the '70s: *Ice Cold in Alex, The Flight of the Phoenix* and that one with the tank – which I think must have been *Sahara*; of course not forgetting *Lawrence of Arabia*. Then later there was *Raiders of the Lost Ark* and even *Mad Max Beyond Thunderdome* (although that was filmed in Australia).

Even after the first Gulf War, the emphasis was still on that dreamlike romanticism of colonial times during the first half of the twentieth century; *The English Patient* was unforgettable.

What I took with me, on all my early and fantastical travels to far off lands, was the image of a young man in brown shoes and a blue jersey, barely out of boyhood, on the trail of some incredible discovery. Hergé's Adventures of Tin Tin has it all in *The Crab with the Golden Claws* (among other titles), and that's who I thought I was, when I stood in a queue at Gatwick Airport in 1989, for my first flight out of my own country. That trip was the first for many reasons and at the end of it I wrote in my journal: 'Best three months of my life.'

PART ONE

Seeking Jerusalem and beyond

CHAPTER ONE:
Land of Milk and Honey

It was a big step for me, aged twenty-two, a bit of an odd feeling as well – standing in that first queue, a hundred of us against the wall, having our hand luggage searched through by security. In 1989, I think it was only flights to Israel that, in any way, resembled a post 9/11 security detail.

My dad had told me that I was going to a land full of the most beautiful women on the planet, while others had said I might get blown up on a bus; there was some reality in both suggestions. A friend and work colleague of mine had been there and recently returned: it was his tales of life on a kibbutz in the baking sun that had inspired me to go out and do it.

Wayne said I was going to have a great time, but I should be prepared to be challenged, as a new dog in the yard, by the young Israeli soldiers keeping an eye on their patch.

Virtually every citizen of the State of Israel gets brought into the I.D.F. (Israeli Defence Force) at the age of eighteen. National service is three years for boys and two for girls; very few are exempt from this duty, or rite of passage, depending on how you look at it. In my experience, some of those young soldiers were arrogant, and some aloof, but many others were open and friendly human beings.

The international courtesies of repeating please and thank-you just weren't a part of the culture; I supposed that it showed a weakness the Israelis didn't want penetrated. They would do things for you, but when they wanted your compliance they just told you.

It was my first time on an airplane and it was a relatively small one, which shook and roared itself along the runway at a speed I'd never been close to; it was an exciting few moments, and then we were off into the night. I found it cramped in that little seat that left very little room for the tray table to extend. Just before we were due to begin descent, I managed to tip my half beaker of water down into my lap and it didn't look good on khaki chinos, exiting the plane and preparing for the immigration procedure.

It was 2am in Tel Aviv on the third of November, but there were still people walking around outside in shorts and vests – I knew I was in a hot country for the first time in my life.

Once in the arrival hall, all the volunteers on this charter flight were gathered together and divided up to be taken to our respective kibbutz destinations. I didn't even know where I would be going to when I boarded the plane and I drew Ramot Menashe, which was a medium sized kibbutz at the tail end of the Carmel Mountain Range.

We had no idea where we were being bussed to in the middle of the night, but the driver had a swarthy teenager sat beside him at the front, and an assault rifle. I said very little during that drive and we eventually arrived at the big vehicle gate that led the way through the tall wire mesh fence. The gate was opened by a short hairy man in a vest, holding an Uzi sub-machine-gun.

We were driven through the complex of buildings before a downhill section of road ended in a rough track. Then it seemed we were being herded down a concrete path into a sort of stony open space, and that was enclosed on both sides by two rows of box-like concrete chalets with flat roofs and very small porch-ways… It was 4am.

I kept a journal all through that trip and my first entry read:

3rd Nov. Fri.
We nine of us, including an Australian couple, a New Zealand woman and a French girl were shown around the kibbutz. I share a room with Brian (the Australian) and Phil, an ex-British soldier, who has lived on kibbutzim for three and a half years. There are some mixed Danish volunteers and three Faroese girls in our area that's just rubble and dust; they call it 'the ghetto'. The rest of the Kibbutz is gardens.

Actually, most of it was farming land, with some workshops and a small water meter factory. But the centre high ground, where everyone else lived, was nicely kept gardens. It turned out that the ghetto was the last area of habitation at the far side of the fenced in settlement. Beyond us was the community dump, and then a valley of bare dirt and chalk, with some limestone bluffs and a stream running through. There was some rough vegetation around the water courses, and the scattered remains of Neolithic and Bronze-Age human activity. There were also some broken bridge pillars in the water, dating from Roman times.

The land grew vines, citrus fruits and avocados; there were flocks of sheep, a dairy herd, a couple of horses and a camel. It was a contentious point amongst the new volunteers that most of us only got to work in the kitchen/dining room, the laundry, or the factory (referred to as *Aram*.) I was lucky, and got to work in the gardens along with Ambritt (the best-looking of the Faroese girls.) Dina was a very pleasant Israeli woman, who made me laugh at the way she instructed me in the work of the day.

I didn't quite fit in with my group of volunteers at the start, or at all really; they were a package, and walked everywhere as a group. I didn't want to be in the flock, also it irritated me that Phil was looked upon, by most of the newcomers, with a respect I wasn't sure he deserved; there was tension brewing between us already.

I would amuse myself after work by going for walks down in the valley and across the hills. I'd come across something new each time I went out: a wild tortoise, a big red land-crab with one large claw and one stunted one; I didn't know crabs could be found ten miles from the sea on a dusty hillside. I saw lizards, a small deer, and just before dusk one evening, at a wide muddy spring, a jackal broke cover from the pampas grass and trotted across an open stretch to lose itself in the vegetation around a nearby stream bed.

There were other types of wildlife out there, like some large rodents (coypu I thought at the time) that I saw grazing near a water course. It was the jackals that characterised where we were though – right out amongst it. Often, just after sunset, they could be heard screeching and mewling (like a slaughter of children), down in the valley just beyond our site. I think they checked out the dump each evening and the sound was unwholesome.

I did get to work in the dining room a bit (during rainy periods) and I found it quite funny; there was this big Danish girl called Iben, she walked around talking to herself as she worked. I was the only English person and it wasn't always easy to understand the others, who were mostly Spanish Americans or Italians.

Marcelo Spinola was a Brazilian medical student from Sao Paulo; he worked for the kitchen and drove the little dairy van called *Jazran*, delivering milk, yogurt etc. all around the commune. Marcelo and I became acquainted when we were both detailed with the job of setting up the public stage affair for an evening performance of some kind.

I spoke no foreign languages and hadn't even known that they spoke Portuguese in Brazil, whereas Marcelo only seemed to have a dozen sentences of English, so we started up a friendship based on teaching each other how to communicate. I found that I could make quite a few friends by learning as much of this language, as quickly as I could; there was a conglomeration of Brazilian students there, as well as some others, recently made up to become Israeli citizens, from Brazil and other South American lands.

The settlement of Ramot Menashe was only decades old; the makeshift wheelbarrows, that had been used to build it, were still spaced out along the edge of the main lawn and painted up as reminders; one of them was just an old wheel hub from a light truck, welded to the frame.

Friday nights were referred to by us as *Shabbat*, although the Jewish day of rest is Saturday, and there was always something going on. Saturday was our only regular day off and all the volunteers would start drinking right after the dinner on Friday evening. We'd all bought alcohol, with the tokens we received for each week's work, from the little shop that was called *Kolbo*.

The *Kolbo* sold cheap beer, wine and spirits, chocolate and… well that's all we ever went in there for.

We'd sit out on the benches down at the ghetto, until the sun went down, most evenings after work. After sunset, on that first *Shabbat*, we were all crammed into the Faroese girls' room for a party they were having. The discos that were held in one of the old bomb shelters every Friday were obligatory: run by some of the young set of the Israeli *kibbutzniks*, it was where we mixed, and they were great times.

The work, in general, wasn't hard and the pay was just pocket-money, but the management were fair and they organised day-trips for us from time to time. I remember the first archaeological tour particularly, with us all crammed into an open trailer that Gabi (the rotund volunteer leader) towed around the hills, behind the John Deer tractor. On the way back up the hill, just half a mile from home, a rain storm caught us up and everyone was drenched. Gabi was laughing from under the shelter of his tractor cab, while we had no options but to just put up with it. One or two of the more fashionable Italian girls didn't find it as funny as us Brits and Danes did.

So Friday night was *Shabbat*, but any night was a party night down in the ghetto, what else was there to do? We held a belated November 5th bonfire on the twelfth; Alan, Jeff and I had built the bonfire by dragging up wood from the dump and we planted it in the centre space, between the two lines of chalets.

The party was well attended, but not very memorable, other than there being an argument towards the end, where it seemed to be me versus the few left over English, who were taking issue over pretty much any view I expressed – with Alan acting as a referee.

I'd never mixed with these city types before and could hardly believe the statements that were coming out. We had things like: 'The gypsies have been criminalised by the state.' 'New Age Travellers have as much right to set up on private land as you have to farm it.' 'The Broadwater Farm riots (where PC Keith Blakelock had his head hacked half way off) were instigated by a fascist police state.' – I suppose I did go a bit far myself, by suggesting various solutions to the world's problems – and when I'm drunk I do have a tendency to offend people who thrive on being offended. It had all started because the Kiwi had thought she had a rat in her room.

Alan and I sat up beside the fire 'til four in the morning, he wasn't a blind reactionist and I think we'd both worked out for ourselves who we were and how that affected the group dynamic. He was a plumber from Gravesend, Northfleet actually, and one of the few volunteers who had actually worked for a living back home. Most of the others were students: the Brits were mostly liberal lefties, the Skandies weren't interested in politics, and I'm sure all the Latin Americans had come from rich families who hadn't got that way by shouting for equality. Only the Russians (of which there were a few) would have known about applied socialism, and they had obviously escaped from it.

Ironically a kibbutz, by its very nature, was a genuine example of socialism at work: as everyone contributed, to the degree they were able, to living an (albeit state subsidized) communal existence. It was communism without the punishment, sponsored by a rightwing government, and it was great. The places were small enough for it to work, but although they were a melting pot of multiple national identities, there was no pretence about the equality of diversity; it was their place and their rules. You didn't have to be Jewish – but it certainly helped if you were. It wasn't an equal society… and that worked okay. People got out of it what they were prepared to put in.

When we'd finished the vodka someone had left behind, Alan turned in for the night. I settled down next to the fire on a bit of scaffolding plank and slumbered 'til six in the morning, when I managed to get myself up to the kitchen to start the day's work.

I think it was the following week that things came to a head with me and my room-mate. Feathers got ruffled during another late night drinking session out by the fire pit, when it was just us Brits still out there.

Phillip was one of those naturally belligerent; over confident males that everyone new wants to be associated with. He was popular with the girls, and that made him popular with the more impressionable younger males around.

The ghetto was Phil's pride land and he didn't like it that I was put up in his room. He was twenty-eight, I was twenty-two and at least as physically robust as he was. I wasn't challenging him, but that's how he saw it, and he was probably right, when a small argument we were having developed into a sticking point that neither of us would back down from. I didn't think it required a dust up, but Phil insisted.

There were only three of us left out there and Al set out the ring in the dirt yard using bed frames. Phillip went straight in for the kill – he was fast and I was a bit taken aback, but I managed to get him into a decent double headlock over the top, and made him tap out, whilst I kept his head pushed into the dirt. We turned in after that and the next morning we were fine.

Alan and I became good friends, we had a similar sense of humour and we were the only ones from our original group who stayed on beyond the first month. He worked in *Aram* with Richard, the bearded theology student. Richard was alright, once I got over his strangeness, intelligent and much laid back; I think he'd smoked a lot of dope while studying for his masters in alternative humanity (or whatever it was he followed.) The only time I saw him start to lose it was when he and I had been chosen for the chicken harvest.

The chicken house set up (with not too much imagination needed) drew parallels with images of a Nazi death camp in miniature. I'd come from a farming background, but I'd never seen it done with the kind of industrial detachedness from any kind of compassionate sentiments, such as we witnessed on that first night in the hanger.

The chickens were 'deep litter' and kept in very tight. They'd spent their time in total darkness in those huge buildings on the edge of the farm. We'd been in there earlier with the two Israelis who ran it, and if they didn't resemble prison camp guards then I don't know. We had to wade through the mass of white feathered bodies to grab a selection of birds to bring out for weighing and checking that, on average, they were ready for killing.

Richard and I had stepped through the sea of meat with as much care as possible, so as not to tread on any parts of the birds. It was difficult, as they were so tight, and being virtually blind, they never moved as we stepped amongst them. The guards just stomped right through, squashing birds and breaking legs and wings without a care; they would all be dead by the following morning, and processed into nuggets and drumsticks, broken bones or not.

That part had been bad enough, but later that evening, when the bright arc lights were switched on and we stood at either side of the first building – it was impossible not to think of those black and white films shot at Auschwitz, to show the efficiency of the process.

Our job was to force the chickens away from the walls and get them to fit within a line several metres in, so that the machine could pick them up. We were bending down and pushing them into the crush, but the guards showed us how it was done, by just kicking them like footballs. We wouldn't do that and were quite horrified by the whole process. Chickens with broken ribs were falling into the mass in the centre section of the building and they just stayed there, injured and bewildered. The poor things were no more than a month old, fed up on high protein and steroids.

Then the big door at the far end opened and what I can only describe as a combine harvester, with foam paddles and powerful headlamps, started driving straight into the middle of the 18,000 bird crush. The product was paddled round the roller and fed onto the conveyer belt that took the bewildered creatures up through the middle of the machine and rammed them into wire crates at the back. The crates dropped automatically when full, one on top of the other.

There were birds' wings caught in the wire gates and others that had got legs trapped in the moving parts of the conveyer – it was horrendous; all the time it was our job to push them closer to the centre once the machine had passed, so it could come back for another sweep.

I thought it was awful, although I had at least worked on farms processing chickens and turkeys back home. Richard, on the other hand, had little or no experience of live food production, and was shouting for the machine to stop every time he saw a bird caught up. It never stopped 'til the shed was empty.

We had seen that a chicken had managed to remain on one of the feed cylinders, unnoticed, as they were all raised by electric winch before the harvester had come in. Once the live collection was done it was just us two left there, with the fifty or so dead birds out in the dust. We quickly collaborated and opened a side door, pushing the poor thing out into the night. Richard chased it across the yard to give it a start out before the guards came back in; it fluttered and ran as best it could in the direction of the track that led to the dump.

Richard came back in, buzzing with self-fulfilment, and I just thought: better the jackals get it than the Druze-Arab truck driver, who had arrived to transport the crates to another place for further processing.

Once the chickens were all loaded we sat down (at 1am) to a meal of fried chicken schnitzel, before going back to pick up the dead… I don't know what the waste meat became. I do know that later on, in the winter, when the sheep were all penned in and knee deep in mud, they were fed every day with a digger bucket full of a mixture of raw cotton, squashed oranges and chicken muck from the shed clear-outs.

Richard and I were told to report back the following evening for more of the same, but we both refused. As we'd been given the day off to recover, we decided to hitch a ride to Megiddo, a small settlement on the edge of the biblical site translated literally: Armageddon.

CHAPTER TWO:
Bible lands

Megiddo is on the plain of Jezreel, where the Book of Revelations warns that the Four Horsemen of the Apocalypse will ride forth to begin the final conflict – I nearly met my own fate there.

While climbing through the rough thorny scrub covering the ramparts to the ruined site, I'd got myself two thirds of the way up and almost stepped on a coil of venom the colour of the hillside itself. The Palestine Viper reared up instantly, and whipped out at me in one movement as I stepped back fast. I turned and leaped away and, as I landed with my front foot, I saw the scaly brown body in that extended S shape, with its head inches from my trailing ankle. I don't care what anybody says about snakes not chasing people: I was there. It was a full sized deadly poisonous snake, intent on sinking its fangs in me, and it dropped through that brush as quick as I could myself on the steep slope.

My body moved so fast, my legs couldn't keep up and I went head over heels, again and again, all the way to the bottom, where I scrambled out of the thorny scrub and my legs took over again to get me clear. It must have been a sight to see: I was dressed like Indiana Jones and all cut and grazed and stuck with needles and thorns.

After a good look around the site, we caught the bus to

Nazareth – all these places we knew about from when we'd first been taught at school: they were just over the next couple of hills and, in the north of Israel, you could see the next biblical site from almost any other one you were at.

The modern looking, and quite beautiful, Church of the Annunciation encased the older shrines of Joseph and Mary, and we had been joined on our pilgrimage by Joan, a staunch Irish Catholic we'd met at Megiddo. She'd been alright on the bus, but when we got through the gates of the church there was something I said that she took to be less than blind commitment to the faith. She turned on me accusingly, saying 'So you don't believe in the Annunciation then!' I had to ask her to explain the word before I could offer any kind of answer; while Richard smiled and I saw him shake his head just a bit out of the corner of my eye.

One of the trips we all went on, in a coach laid on by the kibbutz, was to Rosh Hanikra right on the Lebanese border. There we visited the sea caves and grottos in the chalk cliff. The old broken 1895 railway lines were still there, sagging out over the water, where the chalk had been blasted from under them. The Israelis had blown up the old French railway tunnel in '48 to block the route to Lebanon.

Next stop was the Bahá'í Faith Gardens, just outside Haifa, before the tour of Acre finished the day at the historic crusader port. Everyone was friendly and getting on together; it was a really nice day.

The volunteers were allowed a certain number of days that they could choose to take off per month, so a few of us caught the bus to Haifa one Sunday to spend the day there. The cable car up Mount Carmel was okay, Elijah's cave down below was uninspiring though. We swam off the beach at the foot of the mountain and then drank some beers and ate kebabs. The youth hostel had an eleven o'clock curfew and we had to rush back to get in on time.

On the morning of the following day we caught the bus to Tel Aviv, and then swam out to one of the breakwaters off the beach. The sun was warm and we lay on the beach as if on a regular holiday – I do find the idea of a beach holiday to be a stupid waste of time after the first three hours. What was different though, was that every fifteen or twenty minutes, a military reconnaissance plane would do a sweep of the coast line; I couldn't say if it was reassuring or disconcerting, but it reminded us that we weren't on any regular holiday. The country was into its second year of *Intifada* (Yasser Arafat's Arab uprising) and anything could happen at any time.

The group broke up after a couple of hours and I walked south along the shore – because I wanted to see Old Jaffa, another crusader port and the place where all the oranges used to come from. There were a few clean areas, but mostly it was a slum: dirty, smelly, and the Arabs who lived there were not welcoming. I saw, for the first time, the difference in the way the Israelis lived, as opposed to the lives of the Palestinians; there was a clear economic difference, but also a lifestyle and culture gap.

The Druze Arabs in the north, on the Carmel and Golan heights, were Muslims too, but they weren't involved in any of the politics and insurgency. They could get proper jobs within the State, and were even able to join the IDF. There is no doubt that Israelis hate Palestinians and vice versa, but it's more about politics and survival than religious prejudice and racism.

On Tuesday I was back in the dining room, but felt increasingly unwell as the day progressed. I had a raging fever by evening and was off work with flu for the rest of the week. Whilst still languishing in the room, I began to read from the Old Testament bible that I had got out of the library before. It started out alright, but I just got bogged down by those laborious sections like Leviticus, Deuteronomy and Numbers.

I started to feel better just in time for the two day trip to Jerusalem that the kibbutz threw out as a parting gift for the volunteers, as half of them were due to finish their time the following week.

It was early December and the eve of the second anniversary of *Intifada*. Getting to Jerusalem was a big thing for most of us. It wasn't supposed to be safe to go unescorted, and that was a fair assumption, whatever your politics.

We went to the Church of the Holy Sepulchre, erected in 326 AD to cover the rock of Golgotha where Jesus was crucified, entombed and resurrected. My spiritual experience was degraded when I came up against an irate priest, demanding I buy a blessed candle, right there in the tomb. I was also quite disappointed that the whole rock had been clad in marble, inside and out, so that none of the original form remained to be seen.

The Western Temple wall (the Wailing Wall) was a sight to see, because of its size mainly. It was the Temple Mount, above it, with the shining blue and gold Dome of the Rock, that made the view so spectacular as we came out of the covered streets to look across at the whole site. I think most of us found the orthodox Jews very odd, in their long black coats and wide brimmed hats – weird looking singular dreadlocks issuing from their temples, which hung down in front of their ears. To cap it all, it had been raining, and many of them had polythene covers over their headgear.

Because of the *Intifada*, no shops were open in the Arab quarter when we were there, and there was no life in the street, other than one persistent young hawker who dared to ignore the rule and push his worthless trinkets. It was not how I'd imagined it would feel.

The coach took us from the divided city, down through a deep valley on the edge of the Judean Desert leading to the Dead Sea. The sun was low in the sky as we descended to the lowest point on the surface of the earth. There was no sand, the land was brown with scrubby vegetation, hilly and covered in rocks and stones.

I was fascinated to see Bedouin tents in the dry wadis, with people riding donkeys and keeping goats. These desert camps were more what I had been expecting to see in the Middle East; it was a drab existence, sheltering in caves and cooking on fires of sticks and branches scavenged from the landscape. Their tents were the colour of their animals because they were woven from the hair of their livestock.

We arrived after dark at Ein Gedi Kibbutz, just a couple of hundred yards from the Dead Sea shore. Once the accommodation was sorted out, and we had eaten, I took myself off to find the shore and stare across this amazing mineral lake that surely every child of my generation knew about. It was so quiet, and a little odd, sitting there on a rock of encrusted salt, all alone and staring over to the shore of Jordan. I stayed there a long time, but no epiphany presented itself; so I wandered back up the slope to where I could hear that our group were laughing and drinking. A beer was handed to me and I rejoined my friends.

It was a good time, and all the volunteers were there together: Italians, Danish, French and various South Americans, as well as the original group that had come over on the charter plane from Gatwick, which seemed so long ago.

Alan, Brian, Marcelo and I decided to go for a swim, but it was impossible; all you could do was float and paddle. It didn't taste like any salt I'd ever been near, it was very offensive, and once back out on the beach, it left the skin with a slimy feeling you definitely needed to shower off.

In the morning we were all taken up to the high rock fortress of Masada: the place where, in 73 AD, Jewish Zealots had held out against the Roman army. It was hot and dusty, with fantastic views across the desert and the Jordan Valley.

Back down in the Ein Gedi reserve, a hidden paradise with a natural spring of fresh water, we saw hyrax climbing around in the bushes. These things looked like rodents, but apparently are most closely related to the elephant. Ibex are incredible: tough solid-looking creatures with curved horns, which can run across an almost sheer rock face, and stand there somehow, while chewing at a root they'd spied out.

The remaining part of the trip was a group bathing session, down at the beach, where we floated around, reading the Jerusalem Post and eating sorbet. I did try to dive under the surface but it was impossible, and stupid; I would never have made that mistake if I'd had any idea how painful it was going to be.

Our over-friendly, super-animated Druze coach driver took us back to Ramot Menashe, north through Jericho and the West bank. There was a lot of military traffic through there and not much else. I did love those IDF vehicles, all battered from the stones thrown at them by Palestinian youths. They had machine-guns mounted and wire-catcher poles installed at the front. There was farmland out there, but the road was defended by high wire fences with wide verges along parts of the route.

Once the sun got low it turned into a party atmosphere on the bus; we were drinking, and singing along to the Beatles all the way home. Alison, the dumpy North Londoner, thought she'd found a bosom pal in the moustachioed Arab at the wheel. I advised against her accepting the offer of going for a drink with him at the end of the trip, which affronted her somewhat. The man was clearly a predator and worked hard and fast; by the time we got back to Ramot Menashe he had advanced his offer to $100 a month for English lessons with his family and sex with him. I don't know if that girl was more shocked or insulted about it all, but she didn't go for a drink with him in the end.

My birthday came and went, a few of us drank vodka in my room and it was Richard's last night. The volunteers all had different dates they had signed up to and before most of them went home they wanted to see the pyramids. I'd made a plan with Alison, to meet up with Brian and his wife Julie in Cairo at a specific date and time; I can't explain how I'd ended up with her as a travelling companion, we didn't even like each other much. I suppose she wasn't quite as secure and independent as she made out.

In the meantime, life went on at the kibbutz, volunteers left and new ones arrived. Phil left, a bit surprisingly, to go back to Barnstable for Christmas, he said. He left his Italian girlfriend,

Francesca, waiting for his return – and he took Alan's bank card with him. Al was running out of money and trusted Phil to be back in a couple of weeks, with whatever sum of money he could get out and bring back for him. In the end both Al and Francesca were disappointed and they never saw Phil again.

I seemed to be required to work most days in the *Aram* during December. It wasn't a bad factory to be in: a central yard with enclosed sheds either side, where various stages of the reconditioning process took place. Being chalky soil, the plastic cogs and workings inside limed up quickly. There were sheds for dismantling and cleaning, which involved a sand-blasting machine for the Aladdin's lamp shaped bronze cases; Richard declared that asbestos was in that machine – I don't know, but no-one wanted to work near it. Alan and I worked across the yard in the *villabrato* shed, where the parts were placed in a series of solution tanks to dissolve the lime scale a bit, before they went into a sonic vibrator, which Alan shockingly called 'the final solution.'

Christmas wasn't celebrated on the kibbutz – although the volunteers had planned to get together and sort something out, nothing much came of any discussions we had, because the different small groups all had their own ideas. The night that decided it, ended with the Italians declaring that they were going to the Carmelite Church on the hill in Haifa, for the Midnight Mass in Latin. The Brazilians said they were going to Nazareth, while others suggested we go to Bethlehem; no-one was staying on the kibbutz, that's for sure.

After nothing was sorted, Alan and I built a fire in the ghetto and started getting drunk. We sung carols with the three Danish girls and then went up to Marcelo's house where three new Brazilian volunteers were becoming acquainted. I managed (by accident) to kick over a full bottle of beer in the room, smashing it on the floor, and then dropped Al's alabaster sphinx he'd brought back from Egypt for his mum; fortunately only its nose got chipped. Then we all hit the disco and made ourselves unpopular there.

Christmas Eve came along, and Alan and I jumped into Marcelo's *Jazran* van when he turned up, down at *Aram*. That was it and we bunked off for the afternoon. Most of the volunteers ended up catching the bus to Haifa in the end; we all went our separate ways after agreeing to meet up again later.

Alan and I spent most of the evening in the M.A.S.H pub, drinking and chatting with two American Navy blokes, whose ship was in the bay. We were carting our sleeping bags around, slung off our shoulders on bits of cord we'd found, we might have been a bit loud too. I think some of the others disapproved when we met up with them at 10.30. Anyway, we all walked up to the Catholic basilica where Al and I stood at the back, not understanding any of it, then the Danes and Italians said they were getting a taxi home.

We picked up the Brazilians and looked for somewhere to sleep like a bunch of hobos. It was a cold night, sheltered by the concrete overhang we found and I'm sure our Brazilian friends had never slept out on the street before, but they weathered it well.

We all caught the bus to Nazareth on Christmas morning. At least two of us had bad hangovers and that windy hill road towards the end of the drive nearly tipped my stomach over the edge. After a walk around, including visits to a couple of churches, Alan and I got the next bus over to Tiberius on the

Sea of Galilee. We sat down at a lakeside restaurant and had a lunch of St Peter's fish, expertly grilled, with a beer to wash it down: 'Hair of the dog' Al said, and it worked.

After our Christmas lunch, we paid out to join a pleasure cruise on the water there. It was warm and sunny, not too bright, we could see the snow-capped top of Mount Hermon, on the heights the other side of the lake. It was a Christmas to remember, but then it was over. We got our bus back to Haifa and walked up town to find a tea shop, where Alan blew the last of his money on a slice of cheesecake.

CHAPTER THREE:
City in the desert

I didn't work on Boxing Day; I just packed my bags for Egypt, feeling quite lonely really. I met Alison, as arranged, in Tel Aviv and we stayed at some graffiti fouled youth hostel, populated by pony tailed backpackers. I felt homesick for the first time, and not that keen really. The coach journey to Cairo started badly. This tall, coloured woman in front of Alison immediately pushed her seat right back into Alison's face and refused to budge. It was selfish and arrogant and she lounged out the whole way across the Sinai.

Karma dropped by and somehow a small wallet bag she was carrying dropped off her shoulders at my feet soon after we'd crossed the Suez Canal. I thought it was right that Alison be the one to give it back to her – after she had sweated and despaired a bit – and I passed the small pouch to her, but a suitable opportunity didn't arise and, shamefully the poor woman got off the coach in Cairo without her passport. If I'd had it in my hand, I might have dropped it in amongst the luggage at the end of the trip and made sure she found it, but I didn't have it and I suppose neither of us fancied getting arrested in Egypt for theft of a passport. We vowed to take it to the US Embassy in the morning and hand it in as found property.

We did go there as early as we could, but there was the woman waiting outside the building, so we did a U-turn and came back a little later when the coast was clear. The passport got posted through the letter-box and we drew a line behind the whole business – I'm still sorry about that to this day.

Cairo was a shock to the system, no doubt about that. We'd stayed that first night in a cheap, mosquito-infested hotel room with no windows, sticky walls and only one bed; I took the floor. The hotel proprietor had done everything he could for us with a big happy smile when we'd arrived the night before, including using his teeth to strip the wires down on some electric cable for us; I forget why.

The daylight was bright, but softened by a dirty smog. There was so much going on in the streets and it was all noisy and chaotic. Everyone we met was overfriendly and it was quite fun to start with. We met Brian and Julie (as agreed) at 12 o'clock, outside the British Embassy, then went for cappuccino and posh cakes at the Cleopatra Hotel. Readied for the melee, we hit the street and almost immediately got picked off it and marched into a perfume shop to receive 'Egyptian hospitality.'

There was a framed photo of Muhammad Ali on the wall: 'When Ali came to visit at my shop' we were told – I'm sure there was a picture of Omar Sharif up there as well. The man rang a bell and a burly Arab came in, apparently from the street, with coco cola and frankincense oil… and the psychological extortion game began.

The four of us agreed to take a taxi to Giza, late in the afternoon, but it was dark by the time we got to the pyramids. We'd seen their giant shapes through the gloom on the long approach road; the monuments, being on the west bank of the Nile, don't catch the last light from the city direction and there was no sunset either. Cairo was a massive third-world city in the desert: fascinating, heaving and suffocating in its own pollution; there was no way the sun could shine through a horizon of carbon and dust.

We were able to walk around the complex without too much interference, although the atmosphere would have been better if the sound and light show that ran every night hadn't begun.

The next morning, Alison and I changed hotels for a much nicer place called the Anglo-Swiss; Brian and Julie were also staying there and it had some old time charm to it, without being over budget. The Egypt Museum was a must, of course, and I lined up to view the treasure of Tutankhamen before the doors closed at eleven fifteen in the morning. The others didn't want the hustle of it all. They seemed more interested in comfort and having an enjoyable holiday, than in seeing the sights and gaining some unforgettable experiences; it was frustrating for me, and then in the afternoon we managed to leave the hotel too late to get up the Cairo Tower before sunset! Built on an island in the Nile, and similar to the Post Office Tower in London, it was the tallest structure in Africa until 1971 – certainly the best view-point in the city.

What we ended up doing was hanging around in a café for a while before going to a cinema to see the new James Bond film, *Licence to Kill.* I found it hard to switch from an atmosphere of grinding poverty and neglect to one where you could feel as if you were in any modern city, enjoying 'normal' activities amongst people who weren't about to cheat or abuse you. I think the problem with Egypt was over population – they had one river, the longest in the world, and everyone lived alongside it.

I came down with 'Pharaoh's Curse' on New Year's Eve;

Wayne (from back on the farm) had warned me about this – and the chances of leaking brown water without even realising it! We hadn't even eaten street food and I'd not gone near the rusty water that came out of the taps.

We all bought train tickets for Alexandria, and also for Aswan (in the south) for when we got back from the coast. I bought a plane ticket for Sharm el-Sheikh in Sinai, as my chosen way out of Egypt, instead of taking the bus back the way we'd come. Before leaving Cairo I went back to the pyramids on my own, in daylight this time. I wanted to ride a camel but I didn't have a chance to look for one myself, as before I got anywhere near an animal, I was befriended by a well-dressed little Arab with a sinister grin, who said he would show me where to hire one.

My new friend walked me through a suburb, where I couldn't tell if the square, flat-roofed cement and brick buildings were for people or animals. We came across a turbaned Bedouin who was ordered to prepare my camel, for which I paid; then my friend got on a small horse and told me to pay for that as well.

My camel followed the horse out into open ground, where there were dirty sand dunes and recent building rubble. It was from here that the classic view of the three pyramids could be admired. I tried to conjure up the romantic image of a traveller in time, but I wasn't feeling it, as my friend – who I'm pretty sure had told me he wasn't after money and definitely didn't work at the site – kept trotting us along and stopping beside me to say stuff like: 'Tally ho' and 'Englishman, are you happy.' I would have been much happier if he hadn't kept insisting that I was.

We couldn't stop for more than a minute before some TB riddled hawker in a dusty robe would just appear from nowhere, with a priceless ancient relic in his hand, or some suspicious looking bottle of an unrecognisable soft drink.

Before very long we were back in that dusty grey suburb and the animals were handed to a boy who ran up to us. I said 'Thank-you very much, it was nice meeting you' and started walking off. He asked for *Baksheesh* saying he wanted money for being a guide now. Well, I thought: as he'd lied to me, taken up my time and overcharged me for my camel (not to mention his horse), that I owed him very little. I dug into my pockets and gave him some small notes, amounting to little more than one Egyptian pound; that was the limit of the service he'd provided for me – that I hadn't wanted in the first place.

His grin turned into a snarl as he said: 'What is this? This is *piastres*!' I carried on walking, saying 'Okay, you don't want it' and put my hand back in my pocket. He was furious and followed me along, ranting as he walked. I wasn't going to stop and argue as I didn't feel like I was in a particularly safe environment if things got nasty – and that's how they play it. He wasn't giving up though, so I produced the same notes again for him and he took them this time. It didn't stop the tirade of abuse though; he walked beside me and even in front of me, but I wouldn't miss a step or deviate from my course. He stopped short of physical contact but it still felt like an assault, especially the spitting in front of me part. When it was clear that I was getting close to the public roadway, he changed his tack and instead of ordering me to stop, he was ordering me to go and made a big show of driving me out of his village, cursing me from behind. Then all of a sudden he was gone.

I'd like to have put that cultural experience down to an isolated case of misfortune on the day – a chance encounter that went wrong – it just wasn't though. Egypt was full of such characters and they were just so awful; gap-toothed and dark browed, with intense yellow eyes, either grinning or threatening; there seemed to be nothing in between.

I am a bit of an observer of national traits when I travel, and a physical characteristic I noticed of Egypt's male population was that so many of them seemed to have a dark scar, or odd discolouration at the top of their foreheads and it was always a vertical mark and reasonably central. I never asked how or why, but worked it out some years later when I saw the same mark on the foreheads of men in Pakistan. Surely it is as a result of them pushing their foreheads onto the floor, with a lot of enthusiasm, several times a day – maybe onto a rough reed mat or something abrasive – I have no other suggestion for something, which then to me seemed a weird phenomenon.

Alexandria was certainly nicer than Cairo and had a quite different atmosphere. We'd seen branches of the Nile Delta from the train window and a lot of flat farm land everywhere. I was thinking we might see where some of that water from the longest river in Africa emptied into the Mediterranean, but those mouths must have been a long way from the city and probably inaccessible.

We did see a bit of the Greco-Roman ruins Alex is famous for and we went down into the Catacombs – that's all I particularly remember. The Corniche that runs along the central bay would have been a pleasant walk in the evening, but for the overpoweringly pungent smell of baked urine at any point where there was a kiosk, post or any suchlike structure that offered a place to stop along the way.

It was good to see people fishing off the rocks, it cheered me up a bit to see them enjoying a regular pastime and hopefully getting some dinner for the family too. This city stop was just a diversion before we went deep down into Upper Egypt, I didn't get much out of it really, as everything in the city was just so much hassle.

I wrote this as the entry in my journal for the third of January:

I had a last look around Alexandria, taxi to and from the C15th fort of Qaytbey, paying just over the correct price, which I don't like. I visited the Greco-Roman museum, bit disappointing, got lost again whilst looking round shops.

We all got on the wrong train even though I'd expressed my doubts, but they still wouldn't run all the way to the right platform and we made it with ten seconds to spare.

Back in Cairo I had great difficulty getting to Tahrir Square from Ramses Station; I had to get out of one taxi whilst it was moving, get another to the Sheraton, pay the right money and then jump on a moving bus and stand on the open step to cross the Nile. I jumped off after paying five piastres when they wanted fifteen.

Finally we all got on what was supposed to be the first class train to Aswan – the distance was close to six hundred miles, following the east bank of the Nile, and it took twenty hours.

That train ride was what made the trip, although it was so awful; it was real travelling and we were getting away from mass civilisation and going into the edge of the famed and ancient territory of Nubia: a real place where the people would have negroid features and live in grass roofed mud huts. It would be an adventure like in the films: *Jewel of the Nile* perhaps.

CHAPTER FOUR: River of life

We boarded the train that afternoon and it rolled out of the Ramses II station, slowly, through neighbourhoods so covered in grit, plastic bags, old tyres and rubble that the goats could get onto the flat roofs by running up the slopes of debris piled against the walls of most of the buildings; everything was the same shade of grey. It's the dust and grit blown in from the desert and dampened down by the smoke of car exhausts and industry that builds it up. I suppose anywhere along a railway line turns into a dumping ground too and if the authorities don't clear it out, then it just becomes wasteland with sitting tenants.

Our carriage wasn't so bad, it had benches of cushioned seats facing each other over low communal tables; I wouldn't even say it was uncomfortable, other than the fact I was suffering from stomach cramps. At every stop, the food and drink vendors were allowed on and they passed through the carriages offering their wares. We left that well alone; wisely I'm sure, but during that evening, the train company's official drinks and sandwich man passed through, claiming to offer beer. I had thought that alcohol was not allowed in Islamic countries, in public at least, so I was curious and asked to see the bottle. The man was lightning fast as he whipped the cap off and thumped the brown glass bottle down onto the table in front of me, causing some foam to spill down the neck of it. He turned his back and walked away, apparently unable to hear me calling out, so that it looked like I had bought the drink – he knew what he was doing.

I didn't really want a warm beer full-stop – it was a local brand no-one had ever seen before and, out of curiosity, I took a sip and it was quite horrible. I left it where it was in the small pool of drying froth where the man had put it. I knew there would be trouble… and there was. When the man came back down the aisle to collect the money he demanded three times what a coke would have cost and I refused. He had never been friendly in his manner, but now he was furious and made all sorts of threats. He kept indicating that I would be arrested, by gripping his own wrists as if he were clapping himself in irons.

I stuck to my guns and just kept telling him to take it away – and he did, after another passenger (who claimed to be a police officer) tried to persuade me to pay and then gave up after five minutes. It was a hollow victory for me, as the whole incident meant I wasn't able to even order a cup of *chai* for the whole journey.

I woke in my seat the next morning, in time to get a glimpse of the sunrise over the sugar cane fields that were dotted with palms and occasional mud huts. There were donkeys carrying bundles of cane on their backs, and people working the land, dressed as they had been three thousand years ago.

The train never picked up any real speed: a lot of the time a horse could have kept up with it. I think the pace was dictated by the condition of the track, more than the state of the engine. The rails, which I assume had been laid under British rule, were not lined up too smoothly and the constant da-da-da-dank, da-da-da-dank sound never stopped: it just got faster or slower; you could feel it through the floor of the carriage that rocked and swayed, mostly rhythmically, but occasionally with a series of jolts that would spill your tea – if you had any.

That angry porter was back again, doing his rounds with the trolley, he stopped to glare at me and pointed at the beer bottle stood up amongst the soft drinks, it had a bent Pepsi cap pushed onto the top and was for re-sale.

My stomach cramps were quite bad and I felt like my insides were bubbling and churning, so I went along to find the carriage that had the toilet – there was only one on the whole train, as far as I could tell, and it was getting some use. I noticed that the men, only needing to relieve their bladders, just stood at the open slide door (which was beside the lavatory cubicle) and let it go. I even saw Arabs in robes squatting on the edge of the opening and it didn't matter to them that the same space was never empty of men standing around, smoking or chewing batons of sugar cane, as the carriage rocked and rumbled along through the hazy countryside.

When it came to my turn through the toilet door, just one look inside was enough: I wasn't going in there! Once I'd seen the state of it, I didn't even want to stand nearby – even though the open slide door beside the coupling gave the best view of Africa I'd seen, as the train wound its way south.

We started to pass steep dusty ravines and mountainous desert terrain on one side of the train, with gently sloping irrigated fields and lush vegetation on the Nile side. There were villages made of rough brick, all walled together; they had flat roofs with beams protruding out. It all looked incredible to me because of the very basic aspect and I wondered what the people's lives must be like. Some of the ragged slopes were riddled with caves that had been dug out as homes and there was no infrastructure whatsoever; just survival.

We stopped at Kom Ombo, a city not far from Aswan and famous for a temple dedicated to the crocodile god. It looked small enough to be interesting and I really wanted to get off there. I didn't see any sign of tourism, just the children making faces at the window; they were funny, they showed me the things they had (like pens and pencils) and before the train moved off again, I gave them some chocolate I had brought from the kibbutz. Egypt did have stuff they called chocolate, but it was expensive and not very nice. Those kids ran alongside the carriage window waving to me as the train pulled out with a blast of the horn and I felt quite good.

My need to use the toilet caused me to venture back to the end of that service carriage; I didn't think I could hold onto my guts until Aswan and I rather hoped it might have been cleaned some time that morning since I looked in last. Of course it hadn't been cleaned, not only that, but it was worse. There was a light brown watery porridge slopping around by the step and against one wall. I stepped over and stood in the centre of the enclosed space. I wished it had just been a hole in the floor but no – this was the posh train.

It had a sink on the wall, full of water that looked like chicken stock, no tap that I remember, or paper of course, and a regular western style toilet with a stained plastic seat. I had brought, what I assumed would be, enough paper tissues for my needs, but the seat used up most of it. I'd done a really good job of papering that seat, fit to sit on I thought, and I stood with my feet placed carefully, trousers down, preparing to twist into position without touching the walls and door, or brushing against the edge of the sink with its contents rippling with the jolts coming up from the track.

Just then the train must have entered a stretch of track with a bit of a twist to it and I waited for it to settle, hoping my paper layer wouldn't shake loose – da-da-da-dank, da-da-da-dank, da-da-da… 'Woah!' The carriage lurched one way, then another, causing a wave within the septic basin and a curtain load of foul liquid slopped right onto one side of the toilet seat, all over my papering. I did consider squatting down on the floor, as I could see others had done before me, but the fear of getting the next load from the basin over my back had me out of that place as soon as it was safe to move.

Aswan, for all practical purposes, was the end of the civilised world. There was nothing beyond it that I knew of, other than the Aswan Dam, which held back the flow of the Nile in a gigantic expanse of water. Lake Nasser stretched hundreds of miles, south to the border of Sudan. Across the river to the west was the Sahara Desert, and to the east, beyond the nothingness and dry mountain ranges, you would eventually arrive at the Red Sea.

The day after we arrived was memorable: we all went to the riverside and eventually agreed on accepting a felucca tour of the islands and convoluted channels of the Nile. Our boatman looked exactly as Hergé would have drawn him, dark and piratical, in worn and faded robes and a loose turban; if he didn't have one wonky eye and a gold tooth then he should have done.

Communication was as basic as this man's education had been, but he knew what we all wanted to see, even if we didn't, and that was fine. It was supposed to be three hours, but turned into four, due to getting the boat jammed on a previous wreck whilst sailing us through a narrow channel. The creaking old wooden *felucca* was a wonderful thing, a sort of an Arab *dhow*, very hand made. The sun bleached canvas sail, as the only propulsion, was rigged up to the cracked and crooked single mast, by ropes that looked like his family might have woven them.

We tied up – for the first stop – on the western side of the river, where the hillside was a conglomeration of ancient crumbling walls, terraces and cave tombs. Rather than follow the camel path, Brian and I chose to wander around ourselves, way up the slope of the hill, where we could easily get to and avoid the self appointed guides and vendors we could see waiting further along the trail. After looking around a couple of cave entrances, I decided to climb straight up to the top of the hill where there was some kind of bell shaped monument. I wanted to be on my own a little while anyway and take in the surroundings.

From the top of the hill the land fell back down to the west; it went some way down as a scattering of broken walls and old trails, blown over with sand and grit, before my eyes met what I had been hoping to see – the edge of the great Sahara. That was it, and I was there to see it. Between me and Morocco it was a roughly undulating haze of pale brown, with any evidence of the touch of man dissolving in the couple of hundred yards or so of tumbled stones that spread down to merge with the wide empty space.

Looking back across the channels of the river, there was greenery and life; a lot of silt brought with the annual floods provided a habitat for palms and grasses, as well as all the same staple crops that had fed the region in the time of Jacob and the pharaohs. It looked like a mythical land, a cradle of life in the desert, and I suppose it was. The sun was warm, but there was a breeze up there and I would have stayed longer with my thoughts, but for the others down amongst the terraces – and the *felucca* waiting.

I started to make my way down when I heard shouts and angry voices in Arabic. I could see a turbaned figure making its way purposefully along the trail I was following. He was coming up from the direction of the kiosk I'd bypassed and it was clear he was demanding payment, as he was waving something in his hand that was probably a ticket. I made off diagonally in the opposite direction and he started running.

I jumped off a rock built ledge onto a different terrace to confound him and then I had to think fast. A new irate dervish joining the chase was fast approaching along my wall from another direction: he had a darkly unpleasant expression on his face and he was sure he had me trapped. I couldn't continue in either direction and I was cut off from the boat below me. There was ugly shouting and lots of arm waving, but the lay-out of this place, which was called the Tombs of the Nobles, was a little like a snakes and ladders board and I was able to jump down off my wall and straight away climb another, which some-how put me two terraces below the two Arabs on my trail and on the main track for a home straight.

They were going crazy, cursing and gurgling and then two boys on camels joined the chase from the riverside trail – they were shouting 'Ticket, hey *khawaga*, money!' I ran for the felucca, with the yells of excited children and feral dogs to spur me on; just fifty yards to go, I was down the bank and leaping aboard the *felucca* from the rickety wooden jetty, and our boatman cast off.

The next stop was the Mausoleum of Aga Khan on a sandy hill some sailing distance away. I remember it as a bit of a poor man's Taj Mahal. We showed interest for a while, and the nature of the building prompted a feminist outburst from Alison; she disagreed with Brian's assumption that the Aga Khan's wife probably wouldn't have the right to be laid to rest there alongside her husband when the time came: he'd had it built for himself, not for her.

After a bit more sailing, and visits to some of the islands, including the boatman getting us stuck, we were delivered back to the starting point at the town's main waterfront on the East bank.

We had thought our boatman was okay up until this point and had discussed, amongst ourselves, how much of a tip we might give him. Then he demanded five Egyptian pounds *Baksheesh* for the extra hour it had taken to get us loose from the wreck when he'd got us stuck.

A fierce argument ensued, and the upshot was that we gave him the amount we'd agreed on; no one thought he deserved a tip now. He tried to block our way off, but Brian and Alison were already past him. Julie had carried on trying to talk him down, but he was not letting her get past without us handing over more money; I had to put my arm between them and hold onto a shroud, cutting his movement off, so Julie could get around to the gang-plank. I let go once she was clear and hopped over the gunwale onto the plank, leaving him spitting and cursing until we were out of earshot.

My last day in the far south of Egypt involved getting up at four in the morning to be taken with the others to the reconstructed temple of Abu Simbel.

The two temples were great; the main one was fronted by four colossal statues of the twelfth century BC Ramses II, twenty metres high: two were seated either side of the great doorway that led inside the monument and this is the image that was on the one Egyptian pound banknote. The carved out chambers inside the temple, with walls heavily decorated in relief, stretch sixty five metres deep and are flanked by columns of other marvellous standing statues.

What is as incredible as the monuments themselves is that they all used to be further down in the valley until the dam was built; when the waters rose to threaten the site, that whole section of the hillside was cut up and moved to the top, then reassembled perfectly, inside and out. The smaller temple (which was still absolutely huge) had its doorway flanked by standing statues, which in themselves ranked as some of the greatest stone imagery in the world. It must have been an incredible sight for the early explorers to come across, accessible only via the river itself.

It had taken three and a half hours for us to get there on the desert road, by shared taxi, crossing the Tropic of Cancer line in the doing so. It was hot and cramped and there was nothing to look at along the way whatsoever; I don't even remember any landscape, it was just hard baked stony wasteland. I liked Lake Nasser, even though it shouldn't have been there. It was a waterscape with gently rounded protrusions of land the colour of last year's straw bales. There was no vegetation and the striation marks left by the receding blue waters were interesting. It was desolate and somewhat sterile, but that's what made it unlike anywhere I'd ever seen.

I watched an African snake-eating eagle fly off from a rock, and glide two hundred metres to its next perch, close to the water. I went to where it had taken off from and picked up a blue feather I found there, and I put it in my wallet. It stayed in there for three years until I lost that wallet one day, it wasn't the small amount of money in there that I was upset about losing, it was the feather from an African eagle I'd saved from that place.

Later that afternoon, I was back on the train, second class this time and heading for Luxor and the Valley of the Kings. My train arrived in the middle of the night and so I wandered the narrow dusty streets, looking for somewhere to get myself out of the way. I came across a woman at a street junction who had a little cooking fire going, it was dark and I asked if I could sit down for a while. My budget was almost non existent by this stage; I had a plane ticket out from Cairo, but no spare money for meals or extra hotel rooms. The woman made me a small cup of *chai* and didn't try to cheat me – it cost almost nothing.

I found the Luxor Temple near the riverside street and it seemed to be just the place to retreat into and see out the night. I hadn't gone far inside its colonnaded interior before I almost stepped on a sleeping Arab. I moved around with a little more care after that; I didn't want to wake anyone and I heard snoring from at least two other bodies sprawled out around the complex.

I didn't like it much in there, when I couldn't see what was on the ground. The giant columns, deeply etched in hieroglyphs, rose from disc like plinths and these suited very well as narrow stone benches I could tuck myself up on. I chose one to keep me a few feet off the ground and hopefully away from snakes, scorpions and stray dogs. I did manage to get some sleep there, for about an hour and a half – but then I was aware of something unpleasant. Maybe it was that I dreamed of the feral dogs and then that a dark shrouded figure had settled down beside me. There was no-one there when I looked up but I didn't want to drift off again in that foreboding place.

I shouldered my pack and started to pick my way back through the vastness of the monument. I wrote in my journal at the time about a giant shooting star and how I'd felt as if the signs were warning me away from the place. I was stepping so carefully and trying to breath without a sound, it was four thirty and I was almost too late.

I heard the temple Arabs starting to rouse themselves for first prayers. They were hacking up phlegm, spitting and mumbling and I saw a small fire start up. I felt relieved to get clear of the place and gravitated towards the waterfront walk, where I found a concrete bench up above the bank to grab another sleep before the light came.

My peace was ruined by a man in Egyptian Tourist Police uniform. He was telling me that vagrancy was a crime (I'm sure that's what he meant me to understand) and tapping the oversized bronze police badge on the sleeve of his shirt with a rod of some kind. Then he suggested I would need to give him money, but when that drew nothing from my pockets he became friendly – way too friendly.

He was sitting down beside me on the bench asking questions, which I answered politely, and then he moved on to talking about his hobbies and it was his self professed dominating sexual prowess he wanted to express upon me. He was saying things like: 'I am strong, very strong with the woman.' And at the same time he began stroking the outlines of a shape at the top of his trouser leg. Well this disturbed me somewhat; the waterfront area was deserted, effectively unlit, and I was alone there beside an instrument of the state whose carnal desires were clearly rising. I was up and walking before he could put together another sentence and I didn't look back.

I wandered along the edge of the riverbank looking at the *feluccas* in the growing dawn and a man with (I assumed) his two sons aboard, called out to me and they all waved. They were just setting out from the shore and held the boat steady, offering for me to come aboard. I said 'Thank you, but I have no money.' To which the grinning deviant exclaimed: 'No money no problem, I make you happy and you make me happy.' The young boys of about ten and twelve jigged around beside him with grins a little less sly than his own.

That was it; I had been warned before I went to Egypt that, fair hair and blue eyes, would attract some degree of proposition from a shockingly high percentage of local males. I hadn't expected to be looked on as meat by a police officer and then a fisherman and his kids, one after the other, within the time it takes for the sun to come up.

I found myself a cheap hotel near the train station to dump my gear and went out again; I had to find the ferry that would take me across the river to get to the Valley of the Kings. It was hot in the valley (more like a wide open quarry really) and stifling in the tombs. I felt a little light headed from not eating since after the Nile cruise in Aswan, two days before; it wasn't just about saving money, it was partly that I hadn't wanted to be needing the toilet on anymore trains.

I suppose the tombs were incredible, but they all just blended into one long reel of hieroglyphic art: it was all too much in one go and I wanted to view the landscape, more than I wanted to be under it. I started to follow the trail up to the steep ridge that divided the Valley of the Kings from the Valley of the Queens, but I got accosted by a couple of 'guides' pushing fake antiquities and then there were the donkey men: all before I'd got two hundred yards. I could see more hawkers and unsolicited 'friends' waiting, spaced out on the ridge itself and I just gave up.

Fortunately, I met a Danish back-packer called Thomas in the share taxi back to the river and we teamed up for the next twenty four hours – it's so much easier to shrug off unwanted attention in Egypt if you are not enduring it alone.

I checked out of the Atlas Hotel at noon the next day and then Thomas and I went out to the edge of town to see the famed Karnack Temple – it's the one in the film of Agatha Christie's murder mystery, *Death on the Nile*. It was impressive, even without the atmospherics I'd felt within the similarly styled Luxor Temple.

The Museum was a disappointment, considering this place was the centre of ancient Egyptian civilisation at its finest. Almost every visitor I met during my time in the land of the pharaoh voiced the same thoughts Thomas and I shared: how did such a great civilisation turn into what we were surrounded by? Surely these people inhabiting the greatest river valley in Africa could have no genetic connection to the images carved on the walls of the tombs and the columns of the temples; they didn't look like the same race at all.

I watched the sunset over the Nile for the last time and

wished that I had climbed that mountain ridge to the Valley of the Queens. I made my way to the train station around ten thirty and, what do you know, the train to Cairo was delayed; I had to sit on the open station platform, getting bitten by mosquitoes until four twenty in the morning. It was chilly and I was wearing my army sleeping bag that had arms and a zip at the waist so you could fold the lower part up behind you as a cushion. This item of my equipment saved me from a fair bit of hardship on that trip and others to come.

The train journey was seventeen hours and I was feeling quite melancholy, thinking about how many hundreds of miles I was away from anywhere I wanted to be. With the money I had left there was a choice of food or accommodation and I opted for just enough food to keep me going; I knew I could pig out once back on the kibbutz, and I needed to keep some back for whatever transport I was going to need to get me there.

I don't remember how I got from the train station in Cairo to the small airport on the eastern edge of the city, but I'm thinking I most likely walked. The domestic airport had an all night café and I bought two cappuccinos and two slices of stale fruit cake whilst waiting for my flight, early on the second morning after leaving Luxor. I had been given a jam roll and a small orange by a Colombian kibbutz volunteer on the train, so I wasn't quite starving.

That night in the airport waiting lounge had been terrible – the Arab travellers in there were obnoxious, not from the bottom of the heap of course, but I hated being amongst them. Some had dyed their grey beards orange, which looked really strange. There was a violent disagreement between one robed-up protagonist and a taller rakier individual in western clothing. They were yelling and bellowing at each other and the orange beard was so fired up, he was shaking and bopping around on his feet like a glove puppet. As it got to its most intense level, they both started grabbing at each other's loose fitting clothing; jumping up and down, shaking each other fit to self destruct...It was weird.

I thought that it must be a very serious crime to punch an opponent in Egypt, as I couldn't understand why they weren't doing so. It all eventually calmed down, with the help of some other well meaning passengers intervening, although nobody took sides and it fizzled out into nothing in time.

CHAPTER FIVE:

Road to the Promised Land

The one hour flight across the Eastern Desert, the Gulf of Suez and south coast of Sinai was one of the most spectacular I have ever taken. The plane was a small fifty-two-seater with twin propeller engines; I wrote that it was a Fuoka, maybe that's what was printed on it, but perhaps I meant Focke. As soon as we were airborne, the dusty grey of the outlying buildings of Cairo started to be lost to sight beyond the dusty grey stony landscape and I don't remember seeing a single green thing. The desert became a hazy yellow and before I knew it, there was the western arm of the shallow bit of sea which leads into the Suez Canal.

This sea was shallow enough, down there, apparently, for the water to have been parted temporarily by some phenomenon; like when the water gets sucked away from the land, before being unleashed as a tidal wave. The destruction of Pharaoh's army in the Book of Exodus could have happened in that way, at that place: certainly not across the Red Sea itself, nor the Gulf of Aqaba, as I could clearly tell, by the deepest of dark blue water filling the rift valley trench between Egypt, Sinai and Arabia.

Once the plane got over the Sinai Peninsular the view was astounding, it was all red, brown and grey swirls of bare rock resembling the ingredients of a cake, only part stirred so that the various colours and textures formed patterns. The little plane turned full circle over the southern point of the peninsular named Ras Mohamed. I could just make out the coast of Arabia, but the best thing was the wide stretch of light blue water off the point, which was really a coral apron just before the big drop into the deep cobalt blue.

I got myself just outside the very small place that Sharm was at the time, and I found the coral shelf at a place called Fayroud Village, just a collection of low impact buildings by the beach. Sharm el-Sheik itself could be easily missed and I remember nothing about it, other than the airport being just a runway, with a small baggage handling hall and a single road leading away from it.

The spot I chose to swim from was a point at the far side of the bay. There was no beach, only a rough rocky stretch, several feet above the water, where I could sit on the edge and look down at the fish within the various crevices and caldrons in the coral ledge. I swam over this formation, diving down into the open water where it appeared in places; I was swimming amongst the black and orange coloured fish, and over sea anemones and clams, but I was cautious too, as I didn't want to get near that drop off.

I only encountered one couple of holiday makers, who had come along the trail from the village; there were no other people and no noise either. I dried off in the last of the day's sun and then walked back to the road. I managed to catch a bus just before the sun set behind those rugged brown mountains and that took me north, a fair way along, to a village called Nuweibaa that was about two thirds of the way up the coast towards Israel. The bus had come just in time for me, because the moment the sun had dropped behind those peaks then quite a cold wind whipped up and it wasn't even dark.

At Nuweibaa I was able to buy an omelette, some cheese and hot rolls quite cheaply, as well as hot tea. This was still Egypt, politically, but it just wasn't anything like where I'd just come from.

I walked out of the settlement along the main road a short stretch, then cut out across a flat gravelly plain towards the mountains, finding myself a dry stream-bed to get out of the wind, where I could sleep for the night, ready to stop the bus out of town first thing in the morning – it had been a great day.

It wasn't an uncomfortable night at all; I was lying in this dry gully, tucked up and wearing all my belongings. Night in the desert – any desert – is a cold one, and this was winter; it's been known to snow on the mountains in Sinai, although this is rare. Naturally the cold air, once the sun has gone behind the high mountains, would sink to the base and then be sucked out across the flat plain to join the warmer air out over the sea: because the rocks cool down faster than the water (the reverse happens once the sun rises) you get this flow of cold air.

I was protected in my gully, as although the cool air sank in, the wind just passed over the top. I'd chosen the spot, not only for comfort, but security too: Sinai was a special designated military zone and it was prohibited to just go wandering without an approved guide; it had only recently been returned to Egypt (1982) from Israeli occupation since 1967 after the Six Day war. I was far enough away from the road to be missed by any spotlights or headlamps, but close enough for me to see what was moving out of the village. It did occur to me that snakes and scorpions might find my place desirable too, but

I took that risk.

I woke up just in time to see the sunrise over the mountains of Saudi Arabia, but just too late to get back to the road for the morning bus to the border at Taba. I had checked on the timings the day before and knew I could flag it down on the road as it came out of the village.

The bus I saw heading north out of Nuweibaa was five minutes earlier than I had expected to see it. I heaved my pack on and ran across the rough ground at an angle to intercept my ride, but it picked up speed and was gone before I made it to the road.

I sat down on my pack, beside the road, still wearing my army sleeping coat as the sun's warmth hadn't got through yet. The only traffic passing by for the best part of an hour was a Bedouin Arab on a camel, who stopped to talk and gave me most of a piece of pita bread he was eating. Soon after, a share taxi came by and stopped for me. It already looked to be full, but the driver wanted another fare and so I got in. I had to sit in the centre of the back seat for some reason and foolishly got in still wearing everything. Within an hour it was stifling in there and I was sweating all right; none of my clothes had been washed for over a fortnight and I knew I must have been humming.

The taxi went all the way to Taba – the Egyptian town about six miles from the Israeli town of Eilat. It was hot, but I chose to walk all the same and my lips were dry and starting to split by the time I got there. I bought a litre of sprite, changed up some money, and then bought a bus ticket to Tel Aviv. I had wanted to see Eilat and spend a couple of days at the Red Sea, but I was on a very tight budget and only just had the bus fare cash to get me back to the kibbutz.

It took me all day before I got to Tel Aviv and it was about eight o'clock by then. I bought a kebab and some falafel, and then found myself an alcove at a beachside café that was closed for the night. I made myself a resting place out of a defunct deck-chair and that was me for the night.

It was 5am and still most definitely dark, but there were people around me making a noise. I thought perhaps it was the shop staff, there early to get things moving, but no, it was older Israeli men. They were all undressing and stretching out in preparation for a morning dip; it was still dark! One man started talking to me and said that they were a group who met each morning at the same time, all year round, to invigorate themselves in the sea.

This bloke said he knew Ramot Menashe and, oddly enough, was going there the same evening to meet some friends. He bought me a toasted pita bread sandwich (from a vendor who was just setting up) before they all left for their swim.

I got myself to Haifa, and then back to the kibbutz to a warm welcome from most of the people I was friendly with. I was so pleased to get back to my room (which I had to myself by then) to shower and get into clean clothes. I felt like I lived there and it was my home.

CHAPTER SIX:
Pale green hills

I found that Alan was the only one of the English volunteers still left at Ramot Menashe, and also that he had become quite miserable. There were no party animals left and all the girls at the ghetto were quite demure, respectable young ladies, who didn't want to be around any kind of drunken frivolity.

It was Shabbat the night I arrived, but the disco was closed and the most exciting things going on in the chalets that evening were people making toast over their electric fires. I'd been up against it to make it home for this night and I have to say it turned out to be quite a disappointment.

For the following Friday night, Alan and I prepared a huge bonfire, anticipating that there might be no disco once again. There was one, so we didn't light our fire until we got back to the ghetto after kicking out time – at least the Brazilians still liked to party.

When the bonfire was going, we piled it high with everything we could find: mattress boards, from the spare beds, a big shelving framework and a stack of unfitted doors we found in a nearby shed, our own cupboard doors, a trestle table and Gabi's wardrobe. At 4am it was a raging inferno, visible from half the kibbutz grounds, and a bunch of concerned residents came down to the ghetto to check it out. Fortunately the beds were gone by that time and we (Al and myself) were grilling toast, using what had been one of our squeegee mops as a cooking hod.

So another week went by and we behaved ourselves – until Shabbat night came around again. It was winter season, with lots of drizzle and there was nothing to do after the evening meal but start drinking and wait for the disco to open. We went along to Rie's room; she was the last remaining Dane, not the best looking one, but a genuinely nice person. All Rie's girlfriends were there, being generally pleasant but not drinking. I had a bottle of wine and Al was on the Arak: a rough sort of Israeli Pernod, and the cheapest form of alcohol to be had.

Alan went over the top – again – and I ended up apologising for him – again – before we went off to the disco on our own. It wasn't pretty; I managed to accidentally smash a bottle out of Al's hand the minute we got in there and then he fell on several people and I had to protect him from more than a couple of the *kibbutzniks* who thought they wanted to have a go. He puked up on the floor and then refused to leave, insisting on dancing to the very end.

The bloke running the disco that night was Yaron, but we called him Jesus, I think everyone probably did, because he just looked exactly like the popular image. He was a bit of a hippy type, in his late twenties, I suppose, but he wasn't that meek and mild bloke we read about in school. When things had got a bit physical, Jesus had told the others that as long as I kept a handle on Alan, it was no one else's responsibility.

We were the last revellers to leave the bomb shelter that night and once I got Alan up the concrete steps and out of the shelter door, leaving Jesus down there sweeping up, he got it in his mind to barricade the messiah in with a broken bit of scaffolding plank or something, under the door handle. There was no way the man was going to get out and I don't think anyone would have heard him calling for help. Hilarious as it was, I couldn't let that happen; Jesus was the only one who had shown some tolerance, and I kicked the wooden shoring away, then dragged Al back down the hill in the direction of our community housing.

In the morning: of course he couldn't remember anything, but we caught some funny looks and a few comments when we were in the dining room. This was my final day at Ramot Menashe and being Saturday, it was everybody's day off. There was plenty of time for Alan and I to gather wood for another fire – and so that was what we did once my bags were packed.

It was just the two of us, sitting around outside like outcasts, watching the sun go down and resenting the fact that the girls seemed to be preparing a tea party that we hadn't been invited to. We felt ostracised, but I couldn't blame them. Then Jatziri, the little Mexican girl, came over to us and said, in her polite and selective English: 'Jim, will you come here please?' When I got to the girls' room, there was a bowl full of toast and a cinnamon spread they had made themselves. There were biscuits, sunflower seeds and cups of hot chocolate, all set out for us.

I stepped into the room and they said: 'Jim, this party is for you.' It was so lovely; they presented me with a folded sheet of paper that had all their names and addresses on, with a little note that said: *Jim.. We wish you the best future, success and luck. We have enjoyed your friendship, your attentions and we desire happiness for you; always!* Signed Jatziri, Claudia, Katia, Francesca, Arianna and Maria Thereza.

Later in the evening we lit the bonfire and it was a blazer with the flaring pine needles we'd put on. The Brazilians came down to see me off and it was just so good that when everyone had turned in, I didn't want to go to bed. I put a couple more doors on and burned the remaining sink unit and all the chipboard from the fridge room to keep warm. I stayed out by the fire with my quilt over me and fell asleep.

I woke up sharp, with Jatziri standing over me – she was saying, so sweetly, that I'd missed the bus. I had done that; it was six fifteen already and there was just one minibus scheduled to go to Haifa first thing; it had left at six.

I did manage to hitch a ride out of the kibbutz, I then found all the right connections to get me to Jerusalem – and from there, the only way to get to Bethlehem was to catch a West Bank bus from the Palestinian side of the city.

It was less intimidating than I had prepared myself for, although there was a heavy IDF presence at Manger Square. There were Christian Arabs at the site, as well as international pilgrims visiting the Church of the Nativity. This place was another massive defensive construction, built in 333 AD, over the cave that is identified as the stable.

It was still a cave and the manger itself was a trough, carved into an alcove of the cave. Disappointingly, the birthing place of Jesus Christ was completely clad out in decorative marble with a silver collar in the form of a star, set into a circular hole in its base. It was possible to put a hand down through the silver star, to touch the carved rock of the trough within, but you couldn't see it.

I caught the bus back a few hours later and flew home on the second of February 1990 – to the tail end of a British winter.

PART TWO

Chasing the Oracle

CHAPTER SEVEN:
Valley of the jackals

My experiences in the Holy Land had really given me an appetite for, not just travelling, but experiencing how life is lived on the other side of the wall – any wall. There were things I liked very much and others I detested, about Jews and Arabs, Christians too: I learned to take all the love and hate with a pinch of salt in each hand.

I had met volunteers from many countries in Europe and Latin America and brought back with me a note book with a few pages of names and addresses that were given as offers of hospitality. I decided to start in Mexico, the following December. I would work my way down to Colombia and finally into Brazil in time for carnival. Well I did do that, and I was gone for six months. When I got back I could speak half reasonable Spanish: but that is another story. There were many places I still wanted to see in the Middle East, and I was going back there one day – before it was too late.

Saddam Hussein invaded Kuwait later that year and Gulf War One was unleashed whilst I was in the jungles of Panama and Colombia. Israel was targeted by Scud missiles, launched from the Iraqi desert, and bomb shelters ceased to be used as Friday night discos.

I knew I had to return to Ramot Menashe; I felt an affinity with the place and managed to convince a friend of mine by the name of Del, that a few months in the Land of Milk and Honey was just what he needed. We didn't go through the kibbutz registration system, just got on a plane and flew out there on the fifteenth September 1992.

We arrived after seven in the evening and got the bus to Tel Aviv City. The first thing I did was buy a phone token from a kiosk, and I was immediately reminded of how rude, in a matter of fact way, some Israelis were.

We found a beach bar that was rocking with the free world, and I remembered how I loved to see those army girls in olive drab, out and about with their nail varnish and Uzi sub-machine-guns. We watched the scene for a while over a couple of beers, then staked out a bit of the beach to sleep on – under a shining moon, with the sounds from the gently lapping waves and a group of locals making music and song further out on the warm sand.

The old folk were coming out to exercise and swim, even before the sun came up, and when it did rise, it was quite warm. I got us over to Ramot Menashe by about one-thirty in the afternoon and the first person I came across was an attractive Brazilian girl I'd met in London a year before, at a house where Marcelo had been staying at. I'd gone up there with Alan and we'd all been to a salsa club.

Gabi found us a room, but we had to clean it out first; it was full of crap left over by previous occupants and the porch area looked like it had been used as a dump. The communal shower block needed an industrial effort to make it usable, and for that, Gabi allowed us two days, plus we were allocated a future rest day in lieu.

This was not the ghetto – that place had been revamped,

landscaped, and turned into reception accommodation for the post-Soviet Jewish influx. We were pioneering a new volunteer accommodation block, previously used as a first home for teenage *kibbutzniks* before they went for National Service. Our block was up at the top of the settlement, still outside the gardens and away from the better class of communal society. It was not bad, but in fairness, you could still call it a tip. There was junk left lying around outside and some graffiti here and there.

We had use of the John Deer tractor with a skip trailer attached and, as Gabi had instructed, all the dirty clothes and gear we collected up went down to the dump. It was a great place, that dump; we picked through other people's discarded junk, to glean for ourselves, things that might come in useful over the next three months.

When, the next day, this young Israeli brat called Aviv, came back to his room at the other end of our block, he asked us where we had put everything we'd cleared from the porch area and wash-room. We told him it was all down at the dump and his face went strange. He said: 'That was my stuff! I am going to speak with Gabi.' I'm afraid we couldn't help laughing as it was very funny. Aviv stormed off and we thought we might not have made a friend there; he pulled himself together though a few days later and I don't think he held a grudge. We were friendly enough afterwards; Aviv was one of those kids who never seemed to be far from whatever was going on, he helped to give the place some comedy.

Before being allocated a working position and whilst we had some time on our hands, Del and I walked down into the valley and then got a lift in a passing Jeep, to a neighbouring village called Gillit Nilli, several miles along the dusty trail. We knew we'd have to walk back, but the ride was fun, the young blokes in the Jeep were just like us, free-living fools out for thrills. On the walk back, we took a diversion through some vineyards and I filled my shoulder bag with black grapes.

The sun was setting as we climbed the last hill and I gave a howl to see if any jackals were about. I sort of wished I hadn't, as the individual cries coming back across the valley incited others to join the hunt and home in on the wounded sound I'd made. They must have been running, because that whelping, squealing cacophony grew from a faint echo to something closer than was comfortable, and quicker than you'd bet on – we didn't actually run, but we were quite relieved the back gates weren't far away.

The next evening, being a Friday, was disco night. After the evening meal we went to the coffee bar/library, which was called *Modon*, and there we met up with most of the recent South American immigrants. There was another Marcelo and a Fabien: both from Argentina, Allen from Chile and Jé from Sao Paulo, Brazil. There was a small group of English speaking volunteers who were staying not far from our sleeping block; we didn't have too much to do with them, as they clearly had their own clique that was dominated by three of the girls hailing from Australia, Scotland and Ireland... And did they want to tell you about it! There was definitely an anti English sentiment that we picked up on a few times, and as the weeks went on we tapped into it for some laughs, as they were easy to wind up. The two long-haired English blokes (who were there also) were fine, but they were near the end of their time at the place.

The weekly disco had moved on from the bomb shelter,

into one of the old chicken houses, which had been cleaned thoroughly and fitted out with the name: -Terminal - it was quite good really, and popular enough to draw thrill seekers out from as far afield as Haifa. That was funny, because really it wasn't all that, but as an Israeli friend I knew out there said, twenty-six years later, when we reconnected: 'Terminal was the place where dreams were made and hearts were broken.' He wasn't wrong.

As soon as I got in there, a pretty, young blonde girl (also from Scotland) perched herself on my lap at the bar and started chatting away; she was nice enough, but I don't remember becoming very friendly with her, before she got picked up by one of the young *Kibbutzniks* who had access to the horses.

There was a bit of dancing and I suppose I got quite drunk. I found myself sitting at the bar next to a quite intense, but likeable pony-tailed *socialista* from Arequipa, Peru. Funnily enough, Alfonso Montenegro Soria was telling me about some English, ex-army volunteer, who'd offered to fight him for making jokes about our Royal Family. Well, it turned out that this was my old pal Phillip and he was still around, supposedly coming back some time the next month. Well, I reckoned he would get a bit of a shock when he arrived and found me there again.

We chatted in English and Spanish for some time, and then I staggered back to the block about 4 am and slept for most of the following day.

Monday was our first day at work and Del and I were assigned to the garden, thank Jehovah! We had to get there for five in the morning and then the routine was to drink coffee until five-thirty, when the light came.

That evening, Gabi took the volunteers out to a Druze village called Daliyat al-Karmel, where we had a walk around, ate lamb *shawarma* and ice cream, then some Arab honey cakes and Turkish coffee. The café owner told us he was entering a national arm wrestling tournament in Nazareth soon – him being the Druze Champion. So before long, there I was, sitting opposite him at a table and trying to win the tab for our coffee. I lost, but he gave us the coffee anyway, plus a postcard each, of his family shop.

This village had a mosque and a synagogue, almost right next to each other, which blows the myth about Jews and Muslims being unable to live side by side.

Jewish New Year came on 27th September and there was a big do organised in the kibbutz plaza outside the dining room. About nine hundred people attended and it was a nice atmosphere; though the food was unimpressive and the wine was cheap, our crowd had fun. The two good looking Israeli sisters (the older one we called Miss Swimming Pool) did a dance routine and 'Jesus' (Yaron Goldstein) performed on saxophone. At the end of the dinner, the volunteers were tasked to help with cleaning the tables, and so we commandeered many of the unfinished wine bottles, then we went back to our suburb to play some drinking game resembling tiddlywinks.

A handful of the young Israelis came back with us; they were coming to terms with the fact they were about to be drafted into the Army and some had crew-cuts already, others were sporting long hippy locks and making the best of their last months of peace and freedom. I remember that party well, as I was wrongfully ordered to knock back some disgusting shot – as a forfeit for failing to correctly name a Disney film during the quick-question part of the game. The hippy dude we knew as 'Moses' was there in the bunch, and one of his crowd got so drunk that all he could do was to crawl about on his belly – they didn't make it to the disco that night, which was on, despite it being a Sunday, so that's how it went. At the end of the night I still had a personal stash consisting of six bottles of wine and two thirds of a bottle of vermouth.

The food at the kibbutz was all free and we were eating as much as we could, as often as we could. It was starting to show on me and I didn't like it, so one day I decided to fast for a day. To help with the purge, I took myself on a hike, with the express intention of finding out what was over the far north-west hills.

On the way, I passed through an Arab farmstead, the house was knocked up from all sorts of things, and it had a big pottery urn for water outside the tarpaulin doorway – there was scrap metal all over the place.

There was this hill I'd always been curious about, with two broad white tracks running up it that was visible from the kibbutz. I headed for that, and when I got there I could see that they were tank tracks and it was an army training ground. I slogged on in the sun and when I thought I'd reached about halfway to the sea, on just the one litre water flask I'd brought, I turned south and followed the line of hills for a bit, before deciding to head back. I was going down into a thorny valley, littered with the bones of dead cattle that had been picked clean by scavengers: jackals and carrion birds most likely. I looked up and there was some black winged shape wheeling about there, opportunistic for its next filling.

This was the wrong day to have started my fast, for sure, but my energy held out until I was just a couple of hills away from home. I had always prided myself on my ability to set a course across blind countryside, hills or woodland, and end up just about where I'd planned to reach. Well, this hike worked out just as fine as expected, navigation wise. I'd seen just one other person during the four and a half hours I'd been out in the hot sun – an heroic looking young woman, blazing along a white dust track on a big quad bike.

It was foolish of me to have set out on my own, in the middle of the day, without the fuel to keep me going and only one flask of the water I'd need. I knew it when I got to a valley bottom, the one where I'd seen the jackal by the creek, on that first day's exploring, three years before. I was near to collapsing on that final climb up the track to the back of the kibbutz; my vision was spotty, I felt nauseous and my legs were so weak. It was heat exhaustion – my eyebrows were gritty with crystallised dust and sweat and I drank loads of water once I made it back, then I just slumped onto my bed in the room.

Del told me that Itzak had come for me early in the evening, as my name had been put down for the chicken round-up, I was flaked out and so they'd had to choose someone else.

The very next day, close to twenty young agricultural students from Valencia arrived to spend a month and, as I spoke some Spanish, they were initially put under my charge in the garden. We were raking up stones on some rough ground, to prepare it for the laying of irrigation pipes.

Those students were fun to be with, a little shy at first, but once we'd broken the ice we all became good friends. They invited us to a party at their place on the Friday, to warm up before the disco opened. I was getting cuddly with a girl called Maria, until she suddenly cooled off when Alfonso started making a nuisance of himself. He was a great bloke when sober, interesting and intelligent, but once he got drunk he was a damn liability – I've heard others use stronger words, words that I'm not going to repeat because I liked the man. His father was some *comandante* in the Peruvian navy and I think Alfie was shipped out to the Middle East to get him out of the way for a year or two. He was supposed to be studying bovine ecology and worked in the milking house.

I'd done a stint in the milking house during my previous stay and had been shocked at the animal factory mentality, many of the cows had mastitis and they were just pumped out all the same, into the common vat for high temperature sterilising; cream cheese was always plentiful at the dining room buffet selection and dairy was a large part of the diet there as far as I could see. For a country as small as Israel to be self sufficient when, at anytime without warning, it might need to be, left no room for animal sentimentalities.

Del and I had some free days, and we wanted to get out and see things. We packed ourselves a lot of food from the canteen and first hitched to Yokne'am. From there we got a bus to Haifa and then paid a local taxi driver to take us down the coast to the crusader ruins of Atlit. The site was on a bit of a peninsular where the old walls tumbled down to the sea. Unfortunately, that castle was a military base, surrounded by barbed wire and with guard dog patrols, so we couldn't get near. Too late for us though, it was evening and so we climbed up onto the foundations of some ancient settlement, carved from the rock, which overlooked the fort. We slept out in the open, watching the sun going down into the sea behind the look-out station. It was a big orange ball descending into the haze where the water met the air.

The next step, by bus, was to get to the Jordan Valley and the Sea of Galilee. We made a seven kilometre hike along the valley and up the steep western side, in blazing heat, to get to the twelfth century crusader fortress of Belvoir. We rested only once on the way up, at a place where there was a handful of small olive trees growing around a tiny trickle of water; it was the only shade we found that whole afternoon. After three hours of punishment, we'd made the 500 meters (1600 feet) climb from the valley floor to the top.

The castle was only twenty minutes from closing by the time we got there, but they had a shop where we could buy cold drinks. We took it in turn to sit with the bags eating frozen yogurt, while the other one rushed around, viewing the site. It was quite low profile, in neat order, but the grand view was looking down from the edge, into the wide deep void below that marked the end of the Great African Rift Valley.

We stayed the night up on the bare, open space where the coaches stop and we could see the sun set across the landscape of Israel, beyond the sugarloaf silhouette of Mount Tabor. At first light, we watched the dawn spread out across the bone-dry hills of the Hashemite Kingdom of Jordan.

Walking back down was easy, although it did get hot quite quickly and the air was still. Once back on the valley floor, we caught a bus to a place at the south of the Kinneret, or Lake Tiberias as the inland sea is also called. Yardenit is where the Jordan River flows sluggishly out of the lake and there is a baptismal site you can visit connected with Jesus in the Galilee. I got into the river near there and swam around the bend, out through the opening and into the lake. It was green and rushy all around this point and the water was calm and an opaque blue-green colour. There was nothing there to spoil it and I thought it had probably looked about the same two thousand years ago, and even before the time of Jesus.

Hamat Gader is a natural hot spring resort, used as a spar even in Roman times. The site, situated above the Yarmouk River and immediately below the Golan Heights, is open to the public and connected to a crocodile park. The river itself forms a natural border between Jordan and what had, for a short time, been under the control of Syria. We could see some of the houses in Jordan on the other side and two old iron bridges; one of these was blown up and laid down in the deep gorge between the barbed wire fences and look-out positions of both sides.

The spar was a great place, and with five or six IDF soldiers walking around on patrol the whole time, it felt quite safe, even when the report of a heavy shell shot rang out from somewhere that sounded close. The soldiers weren't worried, so neither were we.

The hottest sulphurous pool (at 42 centigrade/107 Fahrenheit) had warning signs around it, stating that spending more than ten minutes in the water could endanger life! There was a cooler pool as well, and a hot waterfall flowing into a stream, where the stones were covered with a pale blue sulphurous fur. The site included an ancient synagogue and a derelict mosque, also a well preserved Roman baths complex.

That was as far as Del and I went together on that little adventure. By the time we got off the bus at Tiberius on the west shore of the lake, he'd made the decision to return to the kibbutz. It made no sense, as we still had a full day booked off work before the Yom Kippur holiday, during which no-one worked. So that was that and I went on alone.

I got myself to the Arik Bridge on the north shore; this is where the water that becomes the Jordan flows into the lake. It is the run-off from the Golan Heights that is still fresh water as it leaves the 'Yam Kinneret' and only at the Dead Sea does it become undrinkable. It was late afternoon and the area was quiet, I don't remember seeing any other people around. I walked east through the sunset, as close to the shore as I could, and across dry marshland full of wispy bushes and hyrax, I saw deer out there too. There was no road within sight or sound; it was just me and nature, the bronzed green colour of the foliage around me and a comfortable temperature.

I passed an armoured personnel carrier; all shot up, scavenged and abandoned long ago – Israeli or Syrian? I couldn't tell. I walked for two hours and it was completely dark when I came across a picnic site at the beach. I knew I would find a road going out from there, so I chose a wooden bench to sleep on and made a meagre supper of whatever I had left from the food we'd brought.

Waking up, in the open, on the quiet side of the Sea of Galilee was an unforgettable experience. I was sheltered under trees with low fern-like branches and the perfectly still water on the lake surface had a haze hanging over it. The rugged hills turned cornflake yellow as the rising sun touched them. I travelled a fair bit during the early nineties – sometimes with company, but often on my own – and it seemed that the most beautiful moments I was living in would generally be the ones when I was totally alone.

I brewed up some black tea with sugar and then I toasted

muffins over the little camp fire I'd made. When I was ready, I walked along the natural beach for a while to choose a place to take a refreshing swim. After that, I went up to join the road that I knew must be only a few hundred yards away. I managed to get a lift in a minibus and was dropped off at Zemach where the lake joins the Jordan Valley again.

The kibbutz system was like an extended family arrangement: if you lived on one then you could visit any other, and so I walked into Dganya Alef, right beside Yardenit. I'd read about the place being the first kibbutz to be built – in 1910 actually, long before the State of Israel came into being – also that it was the birthplace of Moshe Dayan, the famous Jewish independence fighter, hailed as the hero of the Six Day War in 1967. Some would say he was up there with Ernesto 'Che' Guevara and Ho Chi Minh, although he was a thorn in the side of the British when they were ready to end the mandate. He had been imprisoned, on charges of terrorism and held in the old Turkish jail at Acre, as were other prominent characters who were to hold important positions once the Jews had won their state.

On the lawn, in front of the dining room at Dganya Alef, there was a French light tank just stranded there. It had been captured from the Syrians during the 1948 war of independence – stopped in its tracks by the Jewish settlers using home-made grenades, Molotov cocktails and small bore rifles.

I had my lunch in the communal dining room, then caught a bus back to Tiberius, having completed my circuit of the lake. The last bus I was to take, then got me to the base of Mount Tabor, not far from Nazareth and Afula. I had to walk through the Arab village of Shibli to get myself to the bottom of the zigzag road leading to the monastery at the top.

The Arab Israeli problems are mostly restricted to the occupied territories of the West Bank and Gaza. During the Yom Kippur War in seventy-three, Israel had been attacked on its holiest day (while everyone was fasting for twenty-four hours and praying) by the combined armies of Egypt, Jordan, Syria and Iraq, expeditionary forces also came from Saudi Arabia, Libya, Morocco, Tunisia, Algeria and even Cuba. It was not enough, and Israel, following initial serious setbacks, drove them all out and ended up occupying even more Arab land. The Camp David Accords in seventy-eight led to the return of Sinai, although Egypt apparently declined to accept Gaza back. Israel kept the West Bank and Golan Heights; strategically there would have been no way of holding the state together with those areas insecure.

My point of observation is that the Bedouin people of Shibli can't have hated Jews that much: I was carrying Aviv's army rucksack through a Palestinian village and some of the children greeted me with the Hebrew word *Shalom*. A standard greeting which also means Peace. Older people waved to me and a group of teenaged schoolgirls cat-called me – it was funny because I had actually been prepared for hostility – it wasn't what I was expecting.

The hike up the hill took me half an hour to the top and the view was fantastic. I could see the hill where Belvoir was sited to the east, and the Carmel range to the south-west. I was also able to make out the Horns of Hattin, where the crusaders were defeated by Salah ad-Din in 1187.

There were ruins all across the top of the hill and several caves, all grown over with trees. The recent basilica was quite impressive, built in nineteen-twenty something, with the roof made from marble imported from Italy. The doors were solid brass and the rafters hewn from cedar of Lebanon.

I got talking with Father Andrew, one of the Franciscan monks there; he told me that, as it was the eve of Yom Kippur, there would be no busses now or tomorrow. I should have known that would be the case, but the adventure was more important to me than knowing how I was going to get home, or when. I was given permission to sleep in the grounds, so I chose myself a picnic table under the shade of some trees and waited to watch the sunset. Then I zipped myself into my old army sleeping coat and covered my face to keep the mosquitoes out; it was hot up there that night, but the insects were keen.

I caught the sunrise early in the morning and brewed up some black tea, then I made toast spread with date honey that I'd bought at Yardenit. I liked being at this place, the monks lived a genuine frugal life, an ideal, up and away from it all. They kept chickens for eggs, goats for cheese and a cow for milking. The cow was stabled in an open cave, the way things have been done in those lands for many thousands of years. I felt that I could live like that some time, it would be good for the soul, I thought. The valley down below was full of mist, making Tabor feel like an island. I'd supped on bread and honey and taken only water the night before and I felt like a real pilgrim.

Sure enough, there were no busses, and the only cars that moved were packed full of Arabs who were not going my way. I walked for two hours odd, before getting a lift to a point about three kilometres outside the town of Afula. They wouldn't go to the town; I'd been told that any car that went in would be stoned by orthodox Jews – no one works, eats, drinks or moves about on the Day of Atonement.

I walked right through a ghost town; it was strange, I saw no one on the streets, which were so quiet that I could catch the sound of occasional conversation from within people's homes. The traffic lights were operating still, with only myself as witness, which made it all seem surreal. I walked out the other side of one of the largest towns outside of Haifa – virtually unaware of the thirty thousand odd people living there.

I just carried on walking along this deserted main road; I could see it stretched, in a dead straight line, for ten kilometres across flat open farm land, before reaching the hills. This was the Plain of Jezreel and my route led directly to Megiddo, but as I trekked, the hills just didn't seem to look any closer, even when I'd got half way across. I stopped at that point to take shelter under the only trees I'd come across, where I drank sparingly from my water flask. Mercy came along in the form of a minibus full of *kibbutzniks*, who picked me up and dropped me at the junction for Mishmar HaEmeq: still about a ten kilometre walk from Ramot Menashe, but do-able. I walked for half an hour, up the windy hill road in the midday heat and then, as luck would have it, I got picked up by another kibbutz vehicle and taken right in. A lot of people were amazed that I'd managed to get back from the Galilee during Yom Kippur, I was just happy to be home amongst friends.

CHAPTER EIGHT:
Moral stakes and paper plates

Sukkot is another Jewish observance (a bit like a Harvest festival) and, for this, a celebration was being prepared. As a part of my duties, in preparation for the feast, I was helping with the building of a shelter and palisade out of date palm fronds. During the event there was some singing, as well as the speeches, before we got to share the grapes, sultanas, dates and almonds; coffee and a fruit punch came with it all.

Alfonso had wanted to make a party for afterwards, back at the accommodation block, partly to show *los Valencianos* how we could do things, but also as a bit of a statement aimed at other volunteers to test their sense of humour barriers. Del, myself and a young Israeli named Sharon had worked hard on creating a surprise atmosphere for the event, which would hopefully insult the national sensibilities of just about anyone who happened along, whether they were invited or not. The theme (under Alfonso's direction) was quite daring, and the decorations we prepared so outrageous that we weren't sure how it was going to go down.

After the official evening had come to a close, all the Spanish students wandered over with us to our veranda and I was cringing as I led the way over to our creation – the *Bar La Resaca*. Alfie was already there behind a makeshift bar counter to greet the guests, dressed in a grey suit jacket with matching tie and wearing a crimson fez. We had lighting and the balloons that hung from the ceiling were of course rubber-johnnies, some had even been part filled with milk.

We had prepared an amusing collage poster board from pictures cut out of magazines and we'd added our own captions, with the centre image being a playboy pin-up girl, suitably defaced using a Tipp-Ex brush. Alfie had exceeded himself by writing out, and displaying a drinks list (of drinks we didn't have) that was propped up beside his bar, under a red light-bulb. Every cocktail listed was certain to cause upset to natives of whichever country it was suggested a drink represented.

Our guests looked around expressionlessly and there was very little sound, until their college leader/chaperone suddenly decided it was hilarious. All but two of the students just walked away and we thought we must have gone too far, despite the two blokes left behind saying that the others had only gone to bring alcohol.

We felt a bit silly getting into our costumes, not knowing if anyone was coming back, then stood at Alfie's bar and started to drink the fruit punch laced with anything we had stashed away. Our costumes were unimaginatively made from our own bedding: I was dressed as a Bedouin, Del wore a cowboy hat and had cut a hole in his blanket to make a poncho and Sharon appeared wearing a toga and a laurel leaf circlet on his head. *Los Valencianos* took ages to return, looking a little sheepish, but then the drinks flowed and everyone lightened up. Various friends and neighbours showed up to see what was going on and then it really started to swing.

We'd drunk three buckets full of punch before hitting the disco at about 1 am and it was a wild night. The lovely Maria

Miranda Tarin walked me back to the veranda and we both fell asleep, stretched out on a couch there. We woke around first light and she had to rush back to her dormitory, hoping to save her honour. The poor girl's honour was never under threat and I don't think anyone else was awake at that time to make an assumption.

I, unlike most of my friends and associates back in England, was of the opinion that the newly imposed Poll Tax was fair and correct; that was until I got my letter from them… sent out to Israel for my attention! I never paid it once I'd started travelling and they knocked it on the head in 1993 anyway.

It was Monday 19th October, and time for another jaunt up country. Del and I hitched to Daliyat al-Karmel with a rucksack full of food we'd liberated from the dining room and kitchen the night before. We walked for an hour or so, across the hills and up to the Carmelite Monastery of Deir al-Mukhraqa, which stood on a prominent peak at the end of the high range, just above Yokne'am. I'd wanted to climb this mountain since I saw it on my first trip in 1989. The view was spectacular: Nazareth, Tabor, Afula, Ramot Menashe too. We watched the sun go down over the not too distant Mediterranean and slept on picnic tables outside, below the walls of the chapel.

We had been overeating since we got to Israel, and the food we'd packed for this trip consisted largely of bread and very watery processed meats that resembled hot dogs, beef burgers and chicken nuggets. It was more than we could have reasonably hoped to eat before the heat started to turn it. We'd been trying to eat into this kosher bundle of mush since we got to the hill the day before and I for one had had my fill. Well, there were no toilets at this picnic spot and although I didn't proclaim to be religious, we were in the Holy Land and I wanted to respect that we were camped out on a hallowed hill. I knew I had to release some of that *Dan Meat* – fast – and I didn't want to soil the ground around the monastery. There was nothing for it but to grab one of the paper plates we'd brought along and avoid eternal damnation.

I'd had no idea I was that full, and the plate could barely hold it all. What was I to do then? The picnic site was obviously very popular, as yesterday's rubbish was piled up beside a tree and if there'd been a bin then it was too small. I thought it better to place my paper plate on the top of the pile with another plate covering it, then I thought that whoever cleaned up might not realise the care required when safely picking up the paper plate pudding. So, I wrote a warning sign in large letters attached to the top plate and hoped that the morning cleaner, who we could see making his way around the base of the walls, would recognise the need for caution.

We slunk away, cutting through the bushes to meet the access road and flushing out a large silvery grey animal the size of a modest wolf, I thought, as it flitted through the low cover. The hills were full of jackals, I knew, but I didn't think they grew as big as the creature I saw, in the flash of a second before it was gone. We were able to flag down a *sherut* (share taxi) to get us to Haifa, and then a bus to Nahariya in the North-West. Another bus took us to our planned destination of Miilya in the Upper Galilee, and from there we started our hike to the ruined thirteenth century castle of Montfort, a fortress of the Teutonic Knights of the crusades.

It took us an hour and a half to follow the trail, down to the tree shrouded site on the edge of a deep rocky gorge. We clambered over the giant fallen stones that identified to us the outer edge of the fortification. It had been abandoned for many centuries, broken and largely forgotten. Grown over with bushes and with no road access, it was not on the tourist trail, in fact most people didn't even know it was there.

The complex had been built at the end of a steep finger-like rocky protrusion on the south side of the Nahal river gorge; it was a defensive site, below the level of the land all around, as if it were hiding. The small streams (dry at that time of the year) that ran either side of the finger converged into a fork that joined the main river, deep down below – it was wild and perfect.

Once we'd staked out a base for the night we collected fire wood, and then I went down to fill water flasks from the trickle that had once been a river. There was a steep cut that led straight to the valley floor and a small crumbling fort to guard the water course, which had trees growing from it. It was there that I heard and smelt the wild boar in a thicket. Getting back up was easier than I'd feared, once I discovered the old track that spiralled up behind the ruins and I came back in by the causeway entrance.

So we prepared a cooking fire inside the ruins and with the place completely to ourselves. The sun disappeared amongst the evergreen oaks and, as the light slowly faded, the cries from the woods began. Looking down below from our ramparts into the green, pre-dusk haze, I clearly saw three jackals moving across a slash of semi open ground. I keened my eyes on that clearing for some time and, just before the shapes and colours merged, I was certain I could make out the bulky shape of a hyena, padding across a space were the leaves opened up.

We had two safety aspects to consider: the first one being the proximity to the Lebanese border – we were within range of the missiles that Hezbollah fighters were putting up into Israel on a regular basis, aimed at northern towns and villages; they were inaccurate and indiscriminate. The first Gulf War had brought with it the constant threat of chemical attacks, and everyone in Israel had been issued with personal gas masks back in 1990. This was two years later, but we had still brought our own military surplus respirators from home; I'd brought a complete NBC suit that I picked up at a steam rally, as well as a folding shovel for digging in if it came to it, which of course it didn't.

The more pressing concern that evening was the thought of what might happen when the jackals and hyenas came through the ruins as we slept. We stocked up on as much fire wood as we thought we might need to keep it going all through the night, and then banked it up to a steady little blaze. We heard them, amongst the trees and behind the rocks, even as close as twenty yards, as far as I could tell.

It was a good evening actually, one to remember for a long time. Of course we did fall asleep in the end, but the fire was still smouldering at first light when I woke.

We were up and gone early, walking down stream towards the sea. That river was never anything but shallow, and we saw wild boar on the opposite bank, surprised out in the open for a few seconds before dashing into the undergrowth of the bank. The cliffs were high and rugged to start with, but after close to two hours' walking, we found we were in a gentler valley and the river had actually just dried up, so it never made it to the sea. Israel, being a small country with a high water use, needed every drop of fresh water – you can't transform a desert into a garden by letting it escape into the sea.

We were lucky enough, once we reached a road, to get a lift in a private car, right back to Nahariya. It was an Israeli mother and her pretty teenaged daughter; they said the girl was being called up to do her army service next week and she said she didn't want to go, but she knew she had to – it was more than a little sad – partly because she looked so sweet and innocent, but also for the impossibility of the whole situation and what everyone has to go through out there.

The next bus along the coast road, towards the Lebanese border, dropped us off at a junction with a roadblock installed, at the entrance to a wired off compound on a bit of a rise. This was *Akhzivland*, a self proclaimed independent state, founded in 1952 by the eccentric Eli Avivi. I'd been told about the place and wanted to take a look at one man's aspirations. He'd been arrested for illegally setting up his own state within a country and then taken the government to court in 1971: he won the case and the right to stay there and fly his own flag for ninety-nine years. Yes, he was a strange man… he stamped our passports and we were in.

Most of the half acre of land was occupied by an enormous shambling Arab mansion, which doubled as a guesthouse and museum. It was full of wonderful things, all of which he said he'd found, or dug up on his land. Avivi's state chipped into the northern edge of an ancient Phoenician port town that included a section of beach with the strangest natural rock platforms; they were like formations going out into the sea. The unexcavated site, when we walked along the beach at ten o'clock in the morning, was marred by rubbish, and very determined, shockingly large mosquitoes. The view was good, out to Rosh Hanikra – you couldn't go anywhere in Israel's north and not be able to see something else monumental, not so many miles away.

Del and I stayed at *Akhzivland* for two hours, helping to excavate part of an ancient rubbish dump, from an undercut, where we unearthed pottery, glass and a human tibia. When we'd had enough and didn't really fancy staying in the 'Hotel' with a mad man, we waited on the road for a bus back to Haifa. We then just got transport as far as Yokne'am and set out from there across the hills on a seven mile walk back to Ramot Menashe. I *did* know the way, as it happened; I had done it in the opposite direction back in eighty-nine during my first week out there.

The sun went down long before we made the main road, or the crossing junction to Ein Hashofet and Del was losing faith in my directions. It was a long slog, made more painful for Del by an ankle injury he kept aggravating every time he slipped and stumbled on the loose track-way that I said we should follow. It was so hard for me not to laugh each time it happened, because he was losing his temper and blaming this pair of Hi-Tec trainers he had; I just couldn't see why he kept doing it. I had a blister giving me some trouble too, so it wasn't all about one man's pain; anyway I don't remember him having much trouble the next day back at the kibbutz, so I don't feel too bad thinking about it.

We didn't do badly for trips out that month, as three days later we were all on a trip to Akko (Acre) and Rosh Hanikra. I say all – it was a volunteer trip, in the minibus, but only myself, Del, Katriana (the Irish), Alfonso and a new Danish girl actually went; it was nice though. Alfonso had been drinking heavily the night before and was still drunk in the morning. It was hilarious to see him hanging his head out of the bus window like a sick dog, to try and sober himself up, long dark hair all over the place.

Katriana was alright, on her own, but with the other two, the Aussie and the Scot (we called that trio the 'girls of the British Empire'), it all became obnoxiously anti-British, although, ironically, the only language they knew was English. We only wound them up because they were always craving something to be resentful about.

Our driver, Moshe, was a good bloke; he brought his little girl along too, as there was space in the bus. We all went swimming at Nahariya, then there was food at Acre: pita bread (warm and doughy) with humus, falafel and chips, plus pickled cucumber and aubergine, washed down with bottles of Maccabee beer. I miss all that stuff; I know you can put it all together yourself now from any supermarket, but it's just not the same.

We visited the Al-Jazzar Mosque and the Subterranean Crusader City, then walked through the cobbled streets of the old harbour and the Arab City with its pungent street markets and old charm. There was no menace experienced, no noticeable filth or poverty either. I thought it a far cry from what I'd seen in East Jerusalem and the West Bank last time around.

I'd been told that Phil was back on the kibbutz, but I hadn't seen him until the day after that volunteer trip. He didn't seem to see me when we passed in the dining room, but I saw him, looking a fair bit fatter than he was three years before. He was trying to become a full member and had moved in with an Israeli girl called Yael. I could have destroyed his chances, there and then, but decided to see how things played out. Had he really not noticed me?

Sharon was giving out army haircuts for the boys about to get drafted and I took advantage of this free service too, as my hair was starting to look a bit like a doormat. I hadn't had a grade one skinhead since I was eighteen, but it fitted alright. I perhaps ought to have given some thought to the wisdom of looking like a soldier, just two months before my plan to be in Bethlehem for Christmas Eve.

That night, after the haircuts, the Spanish held a barbecue party at the swimming pool and we all ended up pushing each other in, it was a lot of fun but I left early for my own stupid reasons. They were all going home soon, and so I'd had a good chat with Maria the night before, explaining why I'd kept myself to myself since the toga party. She was alright about it, said she understood but didn't agree. I was trying not to hurt her and all I did end up doing was hurting her, which I never forgave myself for. Many years later, sitting with a beer at the reception bar of a camping park in Catalonia, a woman in her early forties came up to the desk and stood a little way to my side. I kept glancing over and finally I said: 'Maria...*tu nombre es Maria?*' She said 'No' and laughed, then added something about crazy motorcyclists. I laughed too, and ordered another beer.

CHAPTER NINE:
Sahara sands

It was the first of November, and Del and I shouldered our gear, all the stuff we'd packed for three weeks in Egypt. At Tel Aviv, I'd got in touch with an old friend called Yaron, who I'd met in Panama in 1991. We were able to stay at his flat that night and it was good to reminisce a bit about that adventure we'd had, crossing the Darien Jungle, while Gulf War One was going off.

The bus from Tel Aviv to Cairo was a lot more fun than it had been the last time I went that way. On the road across the north of Sinai, people were waving at us from little brushwood villages and also from the top of sand dunes – that hadn't happened before.

As we approached the Suez Canal, we started seeing burned out tanks littering the flat desert, leftovers from the Six Day War. The canal itself was good to see; it was just about sunset time and we took a few pictures, it was really quite narrow, I thought, and I could have swum across easily. There was a mass of vehicles, all grouped around the slipway and jostling for position to get on the transit barge that had taken us across. They were crazy; there was no queuing – horns blaring and throats raw, they just nudged and forced their way into a position where they could cut in.

There were two old Aussie war vets on our bus and they

were dressed, as it seemed, in what they'd worn when they were last here, during the Second World War. It was all big khaki shorts, poplin shirts and slouch hats. They were back on tour after fifty years and some of what they said was historically interesting. These blokes talked the whole way through: about camels and 'bloody natives', it looked like they hadn't been off their outback farms for decades, while the rest of the world was waking up; it was quite funny to see that there were still people like that, but I'd had about enough, long before we got to our destination.

There was an Australian girl called Jenny, on the bus. She was on her own, so we teamed up once we got to Cairo and shared a room for that first night at a fairly decent hotel. It was a bit pricey, and the next day, after registering our passports, we all moved to the Golden Hotel, in Talaat Harb Street; it was half what we'd paid the night before, at six Egyptian pounds. I liked it better, as it was a very traditional, beginning of the century colonial place; almost nothing had been modified since Agatha Christie's era.

I recently read a book called *Dreaming of Jupiter,* by the famous motorcycle adventurer Ted Simon, who also wrote *Jupiter's Travels.* He mentions a place he stayed at in Talaat Harb Street in 1973, which he names as *Golden Hotel.* I wonder now, if they are one and the same. He also describes the wonderful downtown mansion blocks, with small hotels set up on different floors and the ancient hydraulic lift cages that juddered their way up to the reception floors. Well I do remember using one of these lifts during my first stay in Egypt, nearly three years before; I didn't brave it more than a couple of times, as it felt like it was just about to jam, and then maybe even drop down. During this second visit, I did see one or two of those things still installed, but they were no longer working; only gathering dust and waste paper.

Del and I were there for six nights, so it can't have been too bad – breakfast included was sweet tea and rough, stale, gritty rolls with some jam. The milk was supplied in a little brass pouring pot with a side handle that ended up as one of Del's cherished keepsakes.

No sooner had we walked out onto the street from our new place, than we were met by a respectable looking, educated and very helpful Egyptian student, who told us his name was Husain. He bought us tea in one of those shops full of people smoking the water-pipes they called *sheesha*. Then he offered to take all three of us on the bus to meet his family, who just happened to live in the Bedouin district of Giza. It was quite interesting to see this residential area, with its donkeys and carts on the dirt roads, the children and other animals out on the street too. Husain introduced us to his 'brothers' – who didn't look anything like him – and, as if by magic, our student architect friend was gone.

So, we ended up getting ripped off by these camel guides, for twenty Egyptian pounds each (about £4) and that only got us two camels! Del and I had to share, while Sammie the Bedouin made sure he had Jenny up in front of him. He had a turban and that same kind of wilted, jug-like nose as Osama Bin Laden. It was almost worth the money to see how he worked it on her so blatantly, reinforcing the stereotype, and testing to see how far she would let him go. Jenny drew the line at being whipped across the buttocks with his camel switch, although she had been flattered, I'm sure, when he told her he would take her on as an extra wife.

The tour was pretty crap and – at an inflated price – I bought some sandalwood essence and an ornate little glass bottle to decant it into. Once we were done and ready to get a very crowded bus back into the centre, we waited beside the barking crowds of men dressed in bed robes, grabbing for tickets. They'd whipped themselves up into a frenzy as the ticket man stepped out; he had to use a cane to beat them back. There were uniformed police standing by, but they were doing nothing and we had no idea what it was all about.

We were up late the next day and walked to the Khan al-Khalili bazaar; it was a fair way to get to, from Talaat Harb Street, through chaotic streets packed with traffic of all sorts. There were donkey carts, trams and buses, with people spilling out of the doors as they were so full. Women (mothers and their daughters) were selling fruit and bread etc. on the pavement; it was quite a scene. We walked through a meat market and passed many small stalls selling all sorts. We knew we were in the heart of the bazaar when it became so that most of the shops were selling silver and brassware. I bought my souvenir: a little silver teaspoon with the Eye of Horus design, for twenty Egyptian pounds. There were, of course, all the busts of Tutankhamun, as well as the papyrus scrolls, painted with images from the Valley of the Kings.

Before we'd left the kibbutz, we had part filled our rucksacks with family sized portions of dried rice in small polythene bags; these were to distribute to the poor and needy. The recent Cairo earthquake had been on the news before we left the kibbutz and they had plenty of rice there – we obviously didn't ask them if we could give some to Egypt.

So we were carrying these rice portions with us as we walked out towards the suburbs, looking for Old Cairo. A beggar girl carrying her baby brother (we assumed), pushed in on a photo I was taking, so that she could then demand money and Del gave her a bag of rice. I still gave her twenty-five *piastres*, but all of a sudden there were others around us, women and children, who came running for the handouts. We had to walk in the centre of the road to shake off the last of them and a man even came out of his shop to chase some away for us.

Our map showed an area on the eastern edge of the city, marked out as a cemetery, but it was a lot more than that. It was the City of the Dead. There were gigantic mausoleum domes highlighting its silhouette, and collapsed archways punctuated the walled enclosure; it was all crumbling and grey as the dirt in the air. The necropolis covered fifty acres if it covered ten, and amongst the broken monuments and grave pillars were many low, flat-roofed structures. The area looked as if it were an entire medieval city after an atomic bomb had been detonated above.

Walking amongst the graves and tombs, it did become clear that there were people – families – living in the structures there. There was washing hung on lines strung between gravestone pillars that had Islamic inscriptions still visible. There were goats tethered to the same stones, as well as evidence of other human habitation. The people started to appear, as we walked through their yards, and so we gave out the rest of the rice, as well as some spare volunteer clothing we had brought along with us.

The cemetery, as it appeared, had been built during the Mamluk Sultanate, several hundred years ago (C13th – C15th)

and now served as an affordable housing complex for the working poor. The people we met there may have been squatters, but they weren't beggars and we wished we hadn't given out so much of the rice already. We walked right through to the other side and I actually liked the place; the others weren't so keen, as I remember.

A young woman called to us from the gateway of a house at the end of the main avenue when we were almost through. We waved and then she came over and invited us to enter the small enclosure where her family's house was, and where they kept the cows, goats, chickens and ducks. Her name was Samah Afiefy, she was dressed in Western clothes and wanted to practice her English. The older relatives were dressed in typical Arabic clothing and were more like how you would expect to find the people living in such a place. We stayed there for a while and it was fun, no-one asked us for money when it was time to go and we even got an escort out of the cemetery. Del and I went back to visit the family just before we left Cairo and we brought them a big bag of biscuits. The kids helped us learn some Arabic, while their mother cooked us a meal of small fishes with pita bread, we drank tea and answered many questions over the two hours we spent there.

One of the things you must do, if you are in Cairo at the right time, is pay a visit to the camel market. It was on the west side of the river and we had to walk a long way, through the everyday market, along the track of the railway line that goes to Alexandria. That walk was interesting enough on its own; people were selling rabbits, geese, pigeons, turkeys and chickens, amongst other non-food items like heavy-duty bearings etc. We were a little disturbed at the way we saw a woman killing a bunch of quite young chickens: by holding each bird to her mouth and blowing a puff of air into the open beaks – it was worse thinking about it than watching it, as they didn't show signs of panic like I would have expected, just faded away as she held them by their necks. We finally got to the camel market, passing by rubbish tips, dirt and squalor, but also an amazing amount of life: rag and bone men working the narrow streets and quite a lot of regular people just saying: 'Hello' as we walked by.

The place, when we found it, was the absolute image of North Africa, with nomad traders from all over, sporting different styles of headgear. Some of the animals had come from the Western Desert, but many had been brought from Sudan. You could tell the difference from the look of their dark-skinned drivers in robes and turbans; some traders had come from as far as Somalia. There were whips and daggers for sale, as well as coffee and *sheesha* pipe stalls.

It wasn't just camels either; donkeys and some horses were there to be bought, along with carts and also stalls with food, spices, cloth and leather, as well as pots and pans. I bought a David Attenborough style safari jacket from a stall selling clothing that looked like the old uniforms the British left behind.

So much was going on, everywhere: a black skinned boy with South Sudanese features was slaughtering goats, out in the open and there was mess and flies everywhere. I saw a cow walk past a man's shelter, that he'd set up stacked with camel feed, it grabbed a mouthful of the bushy green stuff as it walked by. Two cows wandered into a house through the front door, and were chased out of the back door by a woman who was not amused. A highly prized and clearly pure-blooded Arabian horse was being shown off by its owner in the middle of the square. It was a beautiful animal, well trained and exceedingly expensive. We watched as it performed some fancy steps for the appreciative audience. The whole thing was a great opportunity for taking some really good pictures and I thought I'd got some worthwhile ones.

That same afternoon, Del and I (Jenny took a rest) walked to the northern wall of the old medieval city. We climbed a minaret at the Fatimid Al-Hakim Mosque of the Mad Caliph, and from this vantage point we did actually see some earthquake damage. When it was time to pay 'the guide' who'd showed us up there, we did so, as agreed, then when he asked for 'baksheesh' we gave him twenty-five *piastres* extra. This brought on the most idiotic expression of contrived confusion to his face as he looked from me, to Del, to the money, and then back again.

Bab al-Futuh is one of the enormous city gates. Built in 1087, it has impressive, round towers either side and is connected by masonry to the Mosque of the Mad Caliph. Its massive iron-clad doors were very impressive; dark and terrible looking. We walked east, on the outside of the city wall, until we got to Bab al-Nasra, a slightly smaller-looking gateway with simpler square towers that were no less imposing. When the dusk came down, we re-entered the walled city and walked through the narrow bustling streets. One street was full of open arched workshops, where people were making pots, brass kitchen implements and huge metal trays. Wooden barrels were being made by hand too, and we watched an old man at his bow-driven lathe, making hundreds of little wooden pins for applying that heavy, black eye liner they call kohl. Everything we saw had its own fascination.

We wanted to ride horses, and see the Saqqara Step Pyramid, that was close to twenty miles across the desert, south from Giza. So, the following day, starting from the entrance gate at Giza, we negotiated a slightly inflated price for better horses than those poor old nags in the official government stables. The game started with us riding off through the semi-rural suburbs, where we were then instructed to give up our mounts at another stable and were allocated different ones. It's a shame I don't remember our Egyptian companion, as he was the first guide we'd found who didn't turn out to be a complete asp.

We plodded off along a canal path, passing women washing clothes and cooking pots in the same polluted water. There were donkey carts, of course, and women and young girls carrying firewood. Everything was happening along the canal path, but in a tranquil way; we were away from the motorised traffic and persistent hawkers and the air was cooler than in the city too.

We hadn't gone far, when we all had to make a breakfast stop for the horses at a little village. We were there for over an hour, while we waited in the family home, as we'd been directed. We also got fed whilst we were there; an old man on a donkey brought bottled soft drinks (which we had to pay him for), then a boy appeared with an enormous metal tray on his head; it was so wide that it didn't fit through the door and he had to risk tipping the lot off as he worked it through. The tray held giant flatbreads, some sort of cheese dip and a bowl of coarse salt and pepper. It was good food, but we hadn't asked for it and, of course, we got charged at the end. All the same it was a pleasant enough place to wait while the horses got their fill.

Jenny kept going on about her pony club upbringing and

what an experienced rider she was. It annoyed me, because she got to ride the Arabian mare – it was a beautiful, speckled-grey animal and it held its neck proudly. I wanted to ride it, at least for just part of the day, but she absolutely refused to swap. The horses Del and I were given showed no spirit and just trudged along; they were quite small too and I felt short changed. Del had never been on a horse before and so he was alright about the less than exiting packhorses allocated to us.

Once we left the village, it was off across the open desert. It wasn't quite sand, as you would think of a sandy desert, but more of a gritty, rough, undulating landscape with nothing growing on it – yellow though, and open desert it certainly was. We passed the three small Pyramids of Abusir; they were out on their own, deserted and about four miles from Saqqara, which made a good waypoint.

We had to stop, maybe half a mile from the substantial step pyramid, which I learned was the first of Egypt's colossal tomb structures to be built; it dates back to about 2650 BC. We didn't have tickets to enter the site and so our guide sent some old bloke on a pushbike, off across the desert with our money, to get them. It only cost us one Egyptian pound each, so no-one was making much on the side; I didn't see where he went and I don't know why we couldn't have gone and got them ourselves, but the whole palaver was amusing.

The step pyramid was quite isolated at this site and virtually deserted, although other less well known pyramids were out there in the haze, not many miles away. Every part of the site was covered with dust and desert grit and I liked it better than anywhere at Giza, as there were no tour buses, no noise pollution or plastic bags tumbling in the breeze. It was Egypt as the explorers had seen it in past times. One of the resident Tourist Police tried to make five Egyptian pounds from us each, because we had brought cameras, but he wasn't successful.

We were able to go inside a smaller pyramid and enter a couple of tombs, but the afternoon was running away from us and the sun getting low. It had taken us quite a long time to get out to Saqqara, and it seemed we would be late back – but that was not to be the case.

As soon as we set off back across the sands, something got into the horses. Jenny's Arab was closely escorted by our guide riding beside her – he wasn't going to let it come to any risk. Our two misbreeds suddenly took on a life of their own and they wouldn't be held back once they started. We had no control over them whatsoever – they knew the way back for dinner time and they were taking us.

If you've never galloped a horse across an expanse of desert dunes at sunset, then that's an unbelievable experience to miss out on. They *wouldn't* be stopped and there was no way they were going to turn around for Jenny and her Arab to catch up – not until we were back in the village, at any rate.

There was one Bedouin camp site we had to pass by, a little way on the approach to the village, where a pack of feral dogs, growling and baying for meat decided to give chase. Our mounts kicked up their heels and went for it hell for leather, while Del and I were just trying to stay in the saddle. What a first ride that must have been for Del; if either of us had fallen, then those dogs would have been on us for sure.

Jenny did get to have a trot along with her escort, but we left them for dust and I was so pleased she hadn't agreed to swap – that was a good day to remember.

Jenny left Cairo in the morning and I bought a bus ticket to get me to Marsa Matruh for the following day. Del was going back to the kibbutz too, as he was almost out of money. He was always 'almost out of money.' We'd both brought the same amount from England, but his was nearly gone.

We didn't need the triple room for that last night, so we moved to a double on the floor above; it was under different management and that wasn't the only difference. We had noticeably lower water pressure at the taps, and there was this weird arrangement with one communal toilet seat that you had to bring in from the corridor if you wanted to use it. When you'd finished with the seat, you returned it to the corridor for the guests in the other rooms to use. At least in this new room the windows were not painted white. Having clear glass windows was good, I could see from the reflection in the windows across the street that there was a family living in a shack on our roof and I imagined that they were the hotel staff.

That evening, we were at a soft drink stand outside the Golden Hotel, when a middle-class-looking Egyptian man stopped to talk. He asked us to help re-compose a love letter to his French girlfriend – so we all went to a tea shop and got the job done; it was an unusual, but quite amusing time filler.

Del left at five in the morning for Tel Aviv and I left at seven for Marsa Matruh. It wasn't a bad bus ride: 185 miles from Alexandria, on the Mediterranean coast. I wrote in my journal that evening:

The sea is lovely, the beach is not bad and I was the only one swimming. I realise I left my Clint Eastward hat on the bus...Damn!

The next day Tuesday 10th November, I wrote:

I rented a rickety bicycle; I had to keep kicking the rear wheel spindle every time it slipped out of its one and only working gear. I rode to Ageeba Beach, 25 or 35 km, depending on which guide book you believe. It was quite nice and almost deserted – an islet surrounded by bright yellow rocky sandstone cliffs... beautiful pale blue sea. I climbed around the cliff with my push-bike, where the plateau disappeared and then went over the handlebars riding down off the rock into soft sand.

Marsa Matruh is famous as the place where Rommel chose to be based during his North African Campaign in WWII; apparently he would swim in the sea every morning. There is a place known as Rommel's Isle, it is off a peninsular that faces the tiny port and half of the town. I had to swim across a narrow but shockingly deep channel to get to the place, which ends in a long reef of giant rocks jutting out into the water. A small oblong island sat just the other side of this, it was windy and the waves crashed and boiled over the rocks on the unprotected side. I liked that place a lot, the sea was blue and the land was yellow; I was nowhere near anywhere I didn't want to be and it felt good.

On Thursday 12th I caught another bus, south for three hundred kilometres (the maps stated), deep into the Sahara and quite close to the Libyan border (50 km). It was a four hour drive through mostly featureless desert to the famed Siwa Oasis. There had been herds of free-range camels, out in the sparse scrubland, at the beginning of the journey – and then nothing. This was, at that time, the only road to get there and the buses were the supply lines to and from this ancient outpost, synonymous with Cleopatra, and also where Alexander the Great once came to receive the Oracle.

My bus, which was on a truck chassis, was full of people, as well as big tins of olive oil; they were stacked in the aisle and up on the roof too. There were four other foreigners on board, including a bloke from Rye in Sussex and a girl from Ashford in Kent, just six or seven miles from my home – what were the chances of that!

Siwa town was really quite small, but the oasis area spread out around for many miles. The modern town was a low level spread of modest, flat-roofed buildings sitting alongside the old mud brick town, which surrounds a smooth rock mount. I climbed this rock to get a view of the surroundings, the higher the mud houses reached up the side, the more dissolved and eroded they appeared. On the flat ground at the base, the majority of them were still occupied; they were mostly tall, with small windows and doors and separated by narrow alleyways, where children ran and played. I was told that since the last heavy rains, which swept the area in 1985, degrading the buildings higher up, they had mostly been abandoned.

The medieval fortress of Shali, which rose from the old town, was easily identifiable in its elevated position. It looked just like a sand castle that had been left out in the rain. Of the buildings up on the rise, only the seventeenth century mud brick mosque was still in a usable state. I went back up to the ruins for the sunset at five-thirty, and to witness the call to prayer, given without microphone or loud speakers.

Edward (from Rye) and I rented bicycles for one of the days I was there, to get around the sites that were visible from the central mount. They were all around: wide stands of date palm, lakes and temple mounds. There was very little modern infrastructure to spoil the timeless feel of the place.

It is amazing, I thought, that of all the travellers from around the world who came to Egypt to see the sites – and very few ever got to Siwa – that two of the people on that bus were from my local home towns. Ashford was a small town in 1992, but Rye is still only the size of a large village. I suppose in a place as remote and isolated as this, the travellers who are going to know about it, let alone make the effort to get out there and see it, will be people with a real interest in history, people who read a lot, and Edward did say he worked in a book shop. Another thing about independent travelling is that you are never on your own for too long – not unless you want to be.

We left at first light for our cycle ride that day and found the scant remains of the Temple of Umm Ubayd (Amun). It was only a few large rocks really, but the setting was good, and the dawn sky had reached a nice shade of orange that was complemented by the dark fronds of the date palms. The sun was rising and we hurried on to find the ruined acropolis on the mound of the Temple of the Oracle; the sun rose just as we got there.

It was a sandstone temple perched on the edge of a cliff. From there we could see a wide and shallow lake, surrounded by date palms, and some small buildings that seemed to be made from a mixture of small rocks and mud – like a very coarse concrete.

There are a lot of legends associated with Siwa and its unique isolation. One is that in 524 BC, King Cambyses sent a Persian army of fifty thousand strong, to destroy the Temple of the Oracle and kill its priests. The army never arrived and no trace was left of it. The God Amun so declared that he had buried them in a sandstorm.

There were lots of things to do along the route that we cycled, like taking a swim in a mineral well, known as Ain Tamusi (Spring of the Bride). The Pool of Fatnas was another mineral spring and this one rose from a small island in a large saltwater lake. Siwa is a depression in the Sahara and thus it is an evaporation pan. The scenery on the other sides of the lake was impressive: to the west there were canyon mountains and to the south the Great Sand Sea.

Fatnas Island was full of date palms and we got to it along a causeway and took shelter there from the sun. We picked and ate fresh dates like I'd never tasted before, or since.

Late in the afternoon I rode back over to the two temples we'd visited, to see the difference the light made to the atmosphere. Whilst back at the Temple of the Oracle, I saw a small snake disappear into the stone wall at the base of the acropolis. I don't know what type of snake, it was too fast, but Cleopatra's asp came to mind.

I got to a place called Dacra Mountain, right at the edge of the oasis, and scrambled up to the top just in time for the desert sunset. The scene, over the endless rolling dunes to the south; that was the Sahara everyone thinks of but hardly anyone ever makes it to.

On the way back to my guest house, a wedding procession passed me; the car was all decorated as you might expect. But then four pick-up trucks, crammed full, with about twenty to thirty youths a-piece followed along. They were bibbing horns and letting off fireworks, and then they drove round and round the main square. Fireworks and horns were still going three and a half hours later, in fact it never really stopped all night.

The women, in general, wore long flowing headscarves in black, which they pulled right together across their faces when ever they saw me – or any foreigner I should think; it made me feel awkward but also really curious. I don't know what the women looked like over the age of about ten; all the little ones had fuzzy black hair so I suppose the mothers did too.

I was leaving Siwa the day after the wedding and spent the morning at the Mount of the Dead. It was a hump of rock, pockmarked with simple tombs. The three which had some hieroglyphic depictions on were the tombs of Si-Amon and Mesu-Isis, then one without a recorded name, which contained a human leg complete with foot, and a grizzly head with skin, hair and part of the neck intact.

Edward came along to Marsa Matruh with me, but I left him there the next day when I caught the bus to El-Alamein. There was nothing really there except the war museum and the cemeteries; the British and Commonwealth graves alone numbered 7,367. They were all neatly planted in perfect formation; hundreds of the uniform stones I read bore the inscription: *Known only to God.* The German and Italian cemeteries were signposted as being eight kilometres away, right out of town, so I left it at that and decided to get a connecting bus to Alexandria; three hours was enough for me to absorb the solemness of the place. I knew of El-Alamein since primary school days, when the war games we all played were all WWII inspired. It had been the site of Rommel's defeat in 1942 at the hands of Monty's victorious 8th Army; the tank battle that ended the North African Campaign and probably Britain's greatest win during the whole of the war. I had a Great Uncle in New Zealand who had been in the campaign and I was lucky enough to have talked with him about his experiences in the desert there. 'Yes I saw Monty,' he had told me; there was no doubting the pride in his voice, as he talked about Field Marshal Montgomery affording the Anzac troops an audience.

When I got to Alex' later that day and checked into a cheap hotel, the manager offered me my room for free – if I came with him to the airport duty-free shop. The reason being: Egypt's Islamic code restricted the sale of hard alcohol and the only place that sold it was the airport duty-free shop. Each traveller was allowed to purchase one item and he wanted me to get him a bottle of London Dry Gin. He obviously had a good scam going and it helped me out a little too. The shop put a stamp in my passport to prevent me buying any more on that visa and everyone was happy.

I only stayed one night and whilst there I walked out along the bay to the promontory, where Fort Qaytbey stands. Built in the fifteenth century from the ruins of the lighthouse, that was known from antiquity as Pharos, the fort is a direct descendant of one of the Seven Wonders of the Ancient World. It was quite nice, the old fort – a pastel cream colour, in square form with round turrets – and clearly a popular site for outings, as the courtyard was full of screaming school kids. I went in the museum again, which interested me, as it contained relics from Nelson's victory at the Battle of the Nile. There were plenty of Turkish scimitars too and intricately decorated flintlock muskets.

I caught my train to Cairo later that day and then bought a decent meal to occupy myself, while mulling over my plan to watch the sunrise from the top of the Great Pyramid of Cheops. It was my one and only chance to experience the only fully surviving Wonder, from the original list of seven, in the best way I thought I could.

I took a taxi in the dark, back down to the canal path at Giza and, steering clear of the entrance point to the site, got myself to a place behind the stable block where the official tourist horses were kept. I was challenged as soon as I moved and the man accosting me wasn't going to let me come through, so I bribed him with a small amount of money, which got me across the empty stable yard.

I scrambled up amongst loose rock and rubble to bring me onto a level with the pyramids and within the closed site, where I estimated that the Great Pyramid would be straight ahead. There was an incredibly thick black smog and I could only make out the small, crumbling, part demolished pyramids that I knew were at the eastern base of Cheops. I couldn't see them as a group, but only one by one, as I got to each of them – the visibility was that bad that you could only see what was right in front of you. I knew the layout reasonably well, and as I got to the last small pile of masonry, I knew that my goal was only fifty yards ahead; I still couldn't see this hundred and forty three metre-high, six million ton Wonder of the World.

As I walked forward, I came across a guard hut that was only forty to sixty feet from me when it came into view. I stopped – and I could hear movement along the road that led to it, so I just stepped back a few paces in the gravely sand and melted into the gloom. I wanted to give the night watchmen some space and then approach from a different direction, so I went downhill and to my left, keeping out of sight from the roadway, but close enough to where I thought it was, so as to keep my bearings.

All of a sudden, right there beside me in the murk, was the darkened, but unmistakable shape of the Sphinx, looming ahead of me: twenty-two metres high and eighty metres long; known as Abu'al-Hul – Father of Terror. I had some time to spare and so I went around the side of the crouching monument to get a look at its form, and in the thick black atmosphere it appeared more impressive than in daylight. There were no lights visible, and no colour to the sky at all, but I knew, by the time shown on my watch, that dawn couldn't be too far away.

I knew exactly the direction I needed to follow, the fog wasn't lifting but it was getting less black. I set out up hill again, shadowing the roadway and avoided a group of police and local Arabs who were descending the path; I stopped still and they passed without noticing me. Then I was off again, it was getting lighter by the minute and I stopped by the small, but impressive doorway to a tomb that I had photographed in daylight previously. The entrance was graced by a small sphinx and a pillar either side; it looked secret and dream inspiring in that very strange atmosphere. I made a quick decision to try for a photo (with no flash), but then I was spotted by someone I hadn't realised was staking it out. He called out and I moved swiftly to blind-side him with the shape of the tomb: I hoped he would lose sight of me long enough to confuse which direction I'd gone off in. I could now just see the base of one of the corners of Cheops.

The Arab was following, and when he spotted me again he started shouting and blew his whistle. I had to run, there was nothing else for it – I knew the guards would all be making for the sounds of alarm and I would most likely be trapped alongside the base of the structure. I got around the corner and ran about half way along, as I judged. I couldn't see either of the corner stones or any pursuers, though I knew they were coming. I started to climb as rapidly as I could and the ground disappeared into the greyness. As I couldn't see anyone below, I knew they couldn't see me either, even though I was only three or four blocks up – I'd made it safe.

I could never see more than three blocks above or below me and I just kept going methodically. I hadn't been counting and had no way of telling how far the top was until I was on it. If I could have seen the ground, or even the steep angle of the pyramid's side, then I might have felt some fear as expected. I'd read that many people had fallen to their deaths trying to climb it and I do suffer vertigo; I should have been afraid – four hundred and eighty feet is a long way to tumble.

Many of the square blocks were chipped and sloping a little and they were all covered in soot the further up I got, sort of like a black lichen. They weren't all the same height either, but on average I'd say they were about five feet tall. Up at the top, the air was grey and gritty, it was strangely darker than it had been at ground level too and I could actually see the wind.

I'd climbed along the south western corner edge and in my journal I wrote that it seemed to have taken me only about ten minutes, but it must have been much more than that. I know I was breathless and sweating when I got to the summit at around six-twenty and there was still no sign of the sun. I felt safe enough, as there was a flat area, wide enough to walk around on and a stone on top that carries Napoleonic graffiti. The sides of the pyramid should have been smooth, but the Turks had pillaged all the casing stones and three metres of the top, to help with the construction of Cairo centuries ago.

It wasn't all that nice up there really, I stayed up there, hunched down against the off-centre top stone, for two hours, knowing the sun had risen but seeing nothing – not even a silhouette in the sky – everything was filtered out by a solid grey smog. I actually *watched* the wind flowing up the side from the north and east, depositing the soot from Cairo.

Looking down the steep sides over the crumbling limestone ledges, I could start to see a little of the scale, and around eight-thirty in the morning I decided to make my decent, via the north west edge. The view, as I got further and further towards the bottom, was a little surreal. It got lighter, and everything started looking yellow, including the fog. Then, just like that, I could see the base. Visibility was still so low that when I stepped back up a block, I was sure that I couldn't be seen from the ground. I just listened and picked my moment, as I knew there were people moving around down there. When I judged there was nobody in the immediate vicinity, I quickly scrambled down the last few blocks and I'd made it!

The other pyramids were totally blanked out, so I walked back to the Sphinx and bought my tickets to tour the chambers and passages inside the three main pyramids of Cheops, Chephren and Menkaure (father, son and grandson.) The passages within the Great Pyramid are the only ones I remember now and I really just recall that they were long, narrow, steep and hot. One went up and one went down; the upper one opened out into a high vaulted stairway, leading up to the tomb of the Pharaoh Khufu (Cheops.) There was no fixed lighting and the rocks of the inner walls were dark, probably from oil-burning lamps. There was just a very small, low entrance space to the King's Chamber; the perfectly rectangular room that held the empty granite sarcophagus. The sarcophagus itself was open and had part of a corner chipped off from when the tomb had first been raided, but it wasn't in the centre of the room, as I would have expected it to be. Apparently the measurements of this inner chamber, as well as those of the base area of the pyramid itself, represent a perfect mathematical theorem, worked out by the ancient brotherhood of masons, and it held a great significance. I thought it would be an awful place to be trapped in, dead or alive, and I couldn't wait to get out.

I stayed around the site for a couple of hours and it was at least half-past-ten before the tops of the two biggest monuments could be seen. I never thought that the most iconic setting in the world, one designed around the solar cycle, could have become totally incapable of producing a visible sunrise – or a proper sunset for that matter.

I got a minibus back to Tahrir Square, about midday, then I had to get another bus to a place called Abaniya, to buy a ticket to Sinai for the following day. The buses in Cairo could be chaotic; I saw one stop in Tahrir Square and a crowd of people forced their way on, whilst others were trying to get off. There was a lot of shouting and one old bloke in a turban had got his robe caught up; he was so angry and I saw him raise his staff to strike out at the people – three times – one of them was a traffic cop who had his back to it all and it looked like it was him who was standing on the old man's robe. People were trying to restrain him and eventually he yanked the end of his robe back and went on his way.

Well that was Cairo, twice – and I never went back.

CHAPTER TEN: The burning bush

The Sinai bus took six hours, with the sun gleaming through the windows; I'd foolishly chosen the wrong side. It shone off all the different colours in the bare rock strata. There were yellows, reds and browns laying in striations vertically, diagonally and horizontally throughout the odd shaped lumps and extrusions that made up the scenery alongside the road. There were big mountains too, and I was going to the greatest show: Mount Sinai, also known as Mount Horeb or Mount Moses.

My bus took me to the village of St Catherine, where I bought a good supply of food. Then I walked the two kilometres to the monastery that was tucked neatly into the dry rocky valley at the foot of the mountain. Above the monastery rose some very steep sided crags of pink granite. The sun was getting low in the sky as I came over the shallow pass into the valley and I stopped short of the monastery to find a place to camp out. I chose a spot, just off the track and beside two giant boulders, with a view both into and out of the wadi.

The rocks all around took on an unreal sort of golden-pink hue just before the sun disappeared behind the tall crags. For five or ten minutes, the colours in the sky behind the mountain tops gave the impression of a romanticised image, like the way the sky is represented on some nineteenth century paintings of biblical scenes that you think can't be real.

The Monastery of St Catherine is a Greek Orthodox construction from the sixth century and looks a bit like an old desert fort. It was built around the site where Moses came across *the* burning bush. The bush is still there, they claim; when I did get in to view it I saw an ancient straggle of knurled branch, protected within a walled-in section of the inner courtyard. Anyway, when I got there that Friday morning, the monastery was closed to the public, Friday being the Muslim Sabbath, known as *Jumu'ah*. I climbed a good way up the side of the valley opposite, so that I could get a proper view of Mount Horeb. The zigzag path that wound up from the monastery compound had something of a fairytale look about it and the mountainside was so steep there that I was sure that Moses would probably have chosen an easier way. It's said that the three thousand granite steps leading up to the first crags had been laid there as an act of penance by a single monk in the sixth century. I forget how many years it reportedly took that one man to build his own stairway to heaven.

I started on the Steps of Repentance at one pm. It was hot and I was carrying all my baggage in my rucksack, plus food and water for the night. The monastery had looked like a toy house down below, from the raw gully in the mountainside that got me to the first crags. It took me three quarters of an hour to the first granite archway and then an hour from there to the summit, at 2285 metres. The scenery was fantastic all the way and once I was through the crags I was walking between fingers of red rock all around me, jutting out of the broken waves. It was easy to appreciate that if a man was going to receive the Ten Commandments from God, then this would be a fitting place for that to happen.

It had been hot and still, in the gully, but up on the summit it was surprisingly cold and windy. I had been told to expect a cold night up there, but hadn't been prepared for a chilling three or four hours' wait, before it even got dark.

There was a small granite chapel with a bell outside it, for pilgrims to ring once they had completed their journey. It felt good to ring a chime there, being that I was the first pilgrim that made it up there that day. I wasn't alone though, as there was a tent shelter beside the chapel, where an Arab wrapped in blankets sold me a cup of hot chocolate. He also rented out blankets, but I wanted to rough it out myself, as I'd been doing the whole way through. Most visitors gave the Steps of Repentance a miss and arrived (with guides) via the regular pack route, just to watch the sunset and then go back down. The winding Camel Path uses the rising valley and the shoulder ridge of the mountain, so that only the final section has to be done on foot.

When it came to it, four Australians and three Japanese stayed the night up there with me. I did relent and hire a blanket in the end – for two and a half Egyptian pounds – but it was still punishingly cold. There was one overhang where we could get out of the wind, but it was still only four degrees centigrade (39 f) at five am, according to my old pocket thermometer that ran on a spring. I won't say the granite floor was comfortable either and if I said I'd got an hours' sleep all told, that might have been just a cold hard dream.

Hordes of people started arriving for the sunrise, and Mount Catherine across to the south was the spiritual viewpoint. At 2629 metres, it is Egypt's highest point and it looked like there were three main peaks to it. I observed the silhouettes of three main chapels and one large cross, and from where I was standing at dawn, it did appear that this higher mountain had been touched by God. *For another time* is what I'd written in my journal.

I took the Camel Path back down, as soon as the sun was up. I enjoyed the feeling beneath my boots of smooth granite, worn that way by millions of pilgrims' feet over the centuries. I generated some warmth by jogging as much as I could where the footing was easy and I was down in an hour and ten minutes, it felt almost effortless.

The monastery walls were built for defence and the original method of entrance was by rope winch from a high window; hermits didn't need doors, just a means of hauling up supplies as and when they came. The accessible area within the grounds there was really just an open corridor that led from the magnificent Church of the Transformation, to the burning bush and Moses' Well. The monks themselves didn't impress me; they were rude to me – standing there in the clothes I'd slept in and carrying my belongings – but ingratiatingly welcoming to a group of devout Christian tourists who'd clearly come with pockets full of cash they were certain to leave behind.

The Charnel House was in an outbuilding, fifty yards back up the road towards St Catherine. It held the neatly stacked bones of thousands of previous monks, as well as the dressed and seated, mummified skeleton of St Stephanos. I took a stroll up away from the road and made some tea and a dry luncheon meat sandwich. Then I walked into the village to catch a bus to Dahab: on the Red Sea coast. The bus route offered a change of scenery to a more open landscape, with strange pale knobbly rocks that stuck out of the sand, looking a bit like half melted

Swiss cheeses. The temperature became considerably warmer down at sea level and once there I went to the tourist Bedouin Village with an Israeli called Yohav, who I'd met on the bus.

The village was a complex of many camps, which were laid out in lines of stone huts, to form the enclosing walls to their square gravel yards. The whole thing was very low key, low impact and dirt cheap. The floor of my hut was just gravel, with a mat down on it and a thin foam mattress to sleep on.

I went for a snorkel in the bay, but there was no coral, just lots of litter; I wasn't impressed. I'd heard rave reviews from various travellers about Dahab; people who'd spent weeks at the place, and done not a lot, I suspected. Each night, all the backpackers would drift out to the restaurants, which were all in the same place: square matted compartments, divided by two foot-high walls. In the middle of each 'restaurant' there was a one foot high round table slab for communal eating, with cushions all around and against the dividing walls. It was set up for hippy types to slouch around smoking hashish. The food was great though and I couldn't believe how cheap it was.

On my second day in Dahab, I joined a group of Western travellers on a trip out to the Blue Hole for snorkelling. We all crammed into the open back of probably the oldest and most battered Peugeot 404 in Dahab, for quite a long ride north, to a place where the mountains met the sea. Here the coral started just three metres off the shore, there was no rubbish or infrastructure and we had the place to ourselves. There wasn't a sea bed, it was merely a coral ledge, overhanging the depths of the underwater rift valley. The Blue Hole is just that: a deep blue sink-hole, encircled by coral, that no-one could say how far down it went. It was quite wide, and perfectly circular as

I remember, with multi-coloured fish – some quite large – swimming around the inside coral wall.

The sunset over the mountains made the day, with Venus (the evening star) rising, as all the colours changed. It was my last night, and I spent all my Egyptian money on dinner – save what I needed for the bus to Taba in the morning.

I wasn't likely to stop in Dahab again, if I ever came that way in the future: Sharm el-Sheik, yes, though that little bit of perfection I'd found there three years earlier wouldn't last. I never went back, and now I would be appalled if I saw what had become of it. I think that even ten years later I wouldn't have recognised that little bay, where I first swam in a pristine coral sea. That's the damnation of these isolated little havens, once they get talked about, and if there is an airport nearby, then rapid development can swallow up a dream, and spit it out with the plastic bags and broken glass the morning after: all hail to the rhythm of a hundred generators, pumping dance-trance beats out into streets of neon lights, sullied by groups of hen party revellers from Nottingham. It would be sad to think that no-one ever wonders where all the stars went to, they don't wonder because they never knew.

The bus ride to Taba was enjoyable; we picked up one of the Australians from Mount Moses, at a little place called Bastatas. The scenery was great all the way and I got a good view of the Coral Island with Saladin Fortress built on it, just outside Eilat; one of the classic yachts from the nearby resort was anchored off shore and made for a glorious image.

The Israeli customs and immigration were unfriendly and they only gave me a one month visa; that I hadn't been prepared for. It was the twenty-third of November and so it looked like

I was going to be flying home on Christmas Eve, which hadn't been the plan.

I caught the bus out to Ein Gedi, getting there in the dark and I just wandered down to the shore and staked out a place to sleep, beside the water's edge, and dozed off to the gentle lapping of the Dead Sea. I woke long before dawn and surprisingly there was a light rain falling, so I put two black bin liners over my sleeping bag and settled back down. I didn't get back to sleep and it actually got windy and cold down there, The Dead Sea had woken up and real waves were breaking on the shore.

My plan was to go north to Qumran, where the Dead Sea Scrolls had been found, in caves up there in the dry cliff. So, after waiting an hour and a half for a bus that I thought would come, I started walking. I got a lift to halfway along the lakeside and then waited some more for the bus, which did come eventually, and took me to Qumran at the northern end of the salt lake.

I walked the site with a German girl who got off the same bus and we moved up out of the valley, to the edge of the Judean Desert. It was really quite a beautiful landscape: sparsely dotted with coarse vegetation that the goats and ibex can graze on this time of the year.

It was back through Jerusalem, then Tel Aviv, where I had to pick up my flight ticket, and then I was able to get the straight-through bus to Ramot Menashe.

CHAPTER ELEVEN:
Wolf Castle

It was nice to be back at the place I called home, although it was a little different; there had been a new influx of volunteers: two Danish lads – Jens and Stein, two Canadian girls – Holly and Barbara, then the English couple – Tony and Karen. Michelle (another English girl) arrived about the same time I got back, and maybe it was for that reason that I got on with her better than the rest. Del was there too of course, with his feet under the table as senior gardener and volunteer mentor.

All in all, there were ten of us volunteers living there and this included Phil. He had approached me to size up the situation, one day whilst I was working out on the lawn. After a few home truths, the conversation got interrupted and it was left unresolved – for the time being.

The new group had planned a volunteer party in the bomb shelter for the coming Friday night and it was fancy dress. Like Jé and his girlfriend Keren, Alfonso was actually a student rather than a lowly volunteer, but he almost always turned out for any party going – he came as a Saudi Arab with all the proper gear. Del had the Turkish waiter's suit and I went, quite daringly many thought, as an Orthodox Jew. I went for the full stereotype, with a long dark coat and *kippah* (that little skull-cap they wear). I had pulled out some strands from an old doormat and glued them to my temples as well as sticking some of the wispy fibre to my chin. I really didn't know what kind of a reception I might get from Israelis at the disco, but I thought it well worth finding out if they did have a sense of humour.

The whole thing was a raging success; there were only some people who didn't really see the joke, but most seemed to find it hilarious. I made my peace with Phil that night and I thought he'd grown up some, even if I hadn't. I did get very drunk myself, and when I took to the dance floor I had quite a crowd joining in the fun; as I did cart wheels, high kicks and some kind of inverted scarab dance I invented when I found myself in the crab position. There was a girl called Tally, who worked in the *Aram*; I'd always found her quite imposing and I'd not plucked up the courage to make friends before. Well, we danced like crazy that night and it was great. Israelis really did have a sense of humour.

I soon started putting on weight again and by mid-December I was the heaviest I had ever been. I liked that pizza they made in the kibbutz kitchen every other week. Once, Del and I had taken two lunch sittings, back to back, when we knew it was pizza, and I ate almost two whole catering trays of it; that's about twenty-five individual portions. We couldn't work the rest of the afternoon and had to go and lie down.

One Friday, there was no disco on for some reason, so a bunch of us took the minibus and went to the disco at Dalia Kibbutz, across the valley. We didn't get a very good welcome from their volunteer group, so didn't stay long. Most volunteers were no more grown up than teenagers and, for some of us, it was a last stab at being kids. As an example of childishness: I remember Del and I went to Aviv's room one day whilst he was at work. We turned his electric fire off, his TV on, and put his boots in his bed for a laugh.

The cool *kibbutzniks* wore canvas desert boots, while we had to make do with the aged army surplus boots they gave us, they were so old, the rubber was perished and would come away from the uppers in big chunks after a months' wear. A bunch of us decided to even things up a bit and burgled the equipment store-shed one night. We found a stash of brand new desert boots and took a pair each. It was so obviously volunteers who were responsible, and so I went back to wearing my ruined combat boots with half the heels missing.

Del was out of funds entirely by mid-December and he was going home. You didn't really need money there, as all the food was free and we got pocket money coupons for the *Kolbo* and credit in the *Markolite*. Anyway, he had this fool plan to go back to England and do a load of work so he could get back here before all his friends moved on. Of course it didn't happen; he was living in a dream. There was a send-off for him anyway and Yonite from the garden prepared a cake and some presents, which was nice.

As winter settled in, the land became beautiful again. It was just turning green after the rains, and small flowers like snowdrops were coming out; it was spring before Christmas even, but it wasn't going to be getting any warmer. On the 12th there was a trip out for the volunteers: to Beit Guvrin-Maresha National Park, which was to the south east of Tel Aviv, more or less on a line between Ashkelon on the coast and Hebron in the West Bank. What I remember of this place was the Bell Caves – nine metre high, dome shaped caverns with chimney holes, believed to be the result of quarrying in the seventh to tenth centuries. There were some other caves to look at too, including one used for olive pressing in the fourth century.

We then drove a fair distance east to Soreq Cave: a recently discovered limestone complex, full of stalactites, stalagmites and banks of tiny crystals all over the place. It had been completely sealed away until 1968, when quarrying operations opened up a crack into this magical fairy world. It was pretty good, but visiting the nearby tank museum was a lot more fun; we were climbing all over them like children.

A few days later, I made my last expedition to the north; I was alone on this one and it was a bit of a soul-reading journey. My first stop was Kiryat Shmona, on the western slopes of the Hula Valley and just one kilometre from Lebanon – the town had suffered rocket attacks only a few days before I visited. From there I got a bus to the Banias Springs, on the edge of the Golan.

It was winter and had been dull, damp and cloudy, but when I got to this secluded, tree lined gorge, where springs flow from under a cave in the cliff face, the sun made an appearance and it stopped raining. The water was very cold, and I followed its source to where it joined another small river. The path followed this water course as it wound through the gorge and around the roots of large European type trees like plane, willow, poplar, walnut and mulberry. Many leaves were falling from the trees like it was autumn, while green plants and snowdrops were sprouting underneath as if it were spring. The odd bits of ancient stonework and knurled, twisting old trees bending down over the river, gave the place a Tolkienesque feel and I found myself rushing through it with the energy of a child in a storybook.

The old flour mill was still in service, run by water channelled from the spring, and there was a little Roman bridge with a wooden walkway underneath. Immediately after this, the Nahal Guvta was joined by the faster flowing Nahal Hermon; the Banias River is later joined by the Sa'ar and Dan, to become the Ha Yarden (Jordan River) and that's where the Land of Milk and Honey begins.

I liked that place, and I liked being there alone. I couldn't get a certain tune out of my head while I was there that afternoon; it was *Your song* by Elton John. I had no idea that the words were actually written by Elton's pal Bernie Taupin and when I read in Rolling Stone (years later) that Taupin had said: 'The early ones were not drawn from experience but imagination, and *Your Song* could only have been written by a 17-year-old who'd never been laid in his life' – it made sense, then, for the ballad to be carried on a spirit of completely innocent wistfulness.

There were more bridges, more trees, rocks, torrents and even waterfalls to marvel at. The falls weren't big, by any standards, but being swollen from the recent rains up on the heights made them impressive enough. It was such a nice setting too, and I was thinking I would be looking out for a cave or overhang to make myself a bed for the night. Once I descended the path to the base, I could watch the water cascade from two channels, which were divided by a large boulder at the top; it all fell into a single erupting caldron, spilling a watery mist all around the rocks and tree roots.

On the way back up, I came across a family of five or six wild boar; they were on the other side of the gorge, snuffling around like badgers do. There were some archaeological things to see on another part of the trail, but I took a wrong turn and then decided to go straight up to Nimrod Fortress. Named Qal'at al-Subeiba (Castle of the large cliff in Arabic), it is an Ayyubid castle built by a son of Salah ad-Din.

The path was not well marked on the open hillside and I was aware that the area around the site had been heavily mined by the Syrian Army – twenty years previously, yes, but still a bit of a concern. It took me about an hour to get up the steep hillside to the castle, following animal trails, and when I did get there I found it was enormous. It was well preserved too, for a ruin, It had been occupied in recent times by Syrian troops, strafed by Israeli jets and had even had a 500lb bomb dropped on it during the Six Day War.

It was late in the day when I scrambled up through the massive ramparts and found the place utterly deserted. There was a great view across the Hula Valley to the mountain range above Kiryat Shmona, where I had started from in the morning, but I couldn't see any of Mount Hermon because of the cloud.

The castle was sited on a very steep hill that protruded out from the rest of the mountainside, it divided the beginnings of two infant river tributaries that flowed south: Wadi Nakib to the east and then to the west was the fast running stream of Nahal Guvta, in a deep-cut ravine, filled with stunted trees and thick bushes. This was a truly wild place to stand and look out from and I made up my mind I wasn't going any further that day. There wasn't much time left before it would start to get dark and so I did a little exploration to find a dry place I could huddle up into for the night.

Once I was all set up, I made myself hot chocolate and ate bread and butter for my supper by the light of a candle. I placed my light in an alcove of a bastion tower that looked out across the western ravine. The dark came down and it started to rain again. Then I heard a truly wild ululation – the howl of one solitary wolf – three times it called and there was no mistaking that sound.

I got through the night okay, but stayed in my alcove for the first part of the morning because the rain was heavy. I made some porridge in a mess-tin; it wasn't good, as the oats I'd carried around through Egypt had gone a bit musty. When the rain eased off, I explored the other half of my castle, and the clouds lifted just enough to show me some scant snow cover on the hillside above the village of Neve Ativ, but it was only thinly spread where it disappeared into the cloud line. There was no way I was going to see the snow at the top of Mount Hermon (or anything else) if I did carry on up, so I just watched the eagles or buzzards, soaring over the ruins, as the tops of the walls melted into the thick atmosphere that rose and fell.

It felt good to be walking downhill on the wet road, towards somewhere not so damp. I was wearing most of my own clothing, plus army boots and a green IDF jacket I had picked up at the kibbutz: this definitely helped with hitch-hiking and I got a lift in a newspaper delivery van almost immediately, all the way to Kiryat Shmona.

We had to enter Kibbutz Dan for a delivery; it was a very secure enclosure, with a spiky electric gate covered in razor wire. The whole place was surrounded by high fences, with several rolls of razor wire in between the look-out towers. I wanted to look on the land beyond the border, and so I took a short bus ride to the Druze village of Metula. Metula is referred to as 'the good fence' and its original lands sit either side of the border. Druze only, are able to cross back and forth at this point. The whole village was engulfed in a thick cloud when I got there and I could see nothing other than the queue at the fence. I didn't bother getting off the bus and let it take me back to Kiryat Shmona.

I made some connections south and at the Megiddo junction I picked up a lift, taking me all the way to Ramot Menashe. I was less happy that the refreshing prickly pear fruit, I'd picked from a cactus plant by the roadside there, had left several fine hair-like spines stuck into the roof of my mouth – the red sabra fruit was ripe and delicious, but I'd failed to peel it properly and paid the consequences.

I was pleased to be back in the garden for my last working day on Friday 18th. Yonite, Yossi and Dror had prepared a little going away party for me in the office; it was very nice. There was cake, biscuits and chocolate, as well as a card and little gift. It was where I'd started out from and it was nice to close the chapter there too.

My last *Shabbat* night started with a small party in the bomb shelter. It was with the volunteers and some of the friends we'd all made, and supposed to be a farewell party for me, as well as a welcome back party for Holly. The poor girl had been in a hospital in Haifa for weeks, with Typhoid that she'd brought with her from India. She was clear now and fit to come back in.

For some reason, a truth or dare game was suggested; there was only one dare that got accepted and after that it was all truths. Of course this rapidly degenerated into some increasingly gratuitous questioning, mostly relating to people's sexual exploits. Alfonso quit the game and then Barbara quit the party. It didn't matter though; we were all, by this time, perfectly drunk enough to head out down to the disco.

When I was there in 1989, it was *Lambada* we all went crazy for; the nineties had brought in new styles and now the disco throbbed to *Nirvana* and *Sisters of Mercy.* It was a good last night, and when the disco closed in the crisp early hours, a merry band of disreputables, as well as some of the best young *kibbutzniks*, staggered back up the roadway singing Christmas carols and pointing out the stars. I was about as drunk as I could be without needing to vomit, and I was as happy as I could be too.

CHAPTER TWELVE:
The Holy City

On the Sunday morning, after I'd had a free day to recover, it came for me to say farewell to my second home. I was packed and out of my room; carrying around forty five kilos of assorted mementos and other junk in two rucksacks and a shoulder bag. It was *Hanukkah*, the Jewish festival of lights, and no-one was working; hardly anyone was up as I lugged my gear out to the front gate, where I could get the seven am minibus out. Just as I got to the waiting place and minutes before I was whisked away, I heard a shout. Looking back along the path, I saw it was Alfonso, hair flying all over the place as he ran. I'd only had two and a half hours' sleep myself and he might have had none, but he was there to see me off and that struck me more than just a touch.

When I got to Tel Aviv, I dumped both packs off at Yaron's flat and went on to Jerusalem with just a shoulder bag. The roadside verge gets narrow as it has to pass between hills that close in; there is a steep ravine on one side too. The remains of trucks and armoured cars, left over from the 1948 war, rested in that wooded valley where the road winds its way through. There was still the wreckage of a public bus that went over the edge in 1989, killing everyone in it, when a Palestinian had grabbed the wheel and deliberately forced it over the edge.

I arrived at the main bus station in the modern western

district and it was not far to walk to the old city walls; I had all day to spare, and wanted to view it from around the outside of the walls, before entering the Holy City. The Kidron Valley falls away from the walls between the Temple Mount and the Mount of Olives, so I walked down between the rock-carved mausoleums of Absalom's Pillar and the Tomb of Zechariah. A few hundred yards further down was the Palestinian village of Silwan, where the people who lived there had incorporated some of the caves in the valley walls into their settlement. It wasn't nice down there, far more primitive than any other Arab villages I'd seen in and around the territories and I didn't linger.

The Jewish Cemetery on the Mount of Olives afforded a very good view across the old city that seemed to tilt towards it. I studied some of the stones there and the dates on many of them were significant: 1948, 1967 and 1973 were well represented. There were also some notable Jewish American names with very recent dates, showing the depth of feeling the Mount still generates within the Jewish diaspora. I could also see the hills of Jordan in the distance and it made me think again about how near all these places were and how difficult, if not impossible, it must surely be to harmonise the situation here, with such a crush of passion and injury felt by a population with no choice but to live so closely beside each other.

Up on top of the Mount was the Church of Mary Magdalene, built in 1888 by Tsar Alexander III, whereas down at the foot sits the Garden of Gethsemane. Olive trees live many hundreds of years and some of the knurled old trunks that were in this ancient olive garden could well have been growing there two thousand years ago.

I read somewhere that the Golden Gate – the one Jesus

entered on the back of a donkey – which has been blocked up for centuries, will be reopened at the time of the Second Coming. That was supposed to have been around the end of the Millennium. So the Christians waited in vain for their rapture and the world has moved on: I'm not so sure the faith is still there in the way people felt it in the final decades. In 1992 so much seemed possible, even to a lot of people who weren't exactly religious.

It was through St Stephen's Gate, also called the Lion's Gate, that I entered the city. Jerusalem is as old as the written word, but its present walls were built by Suleiman the Magnificent, four hundred years ago. *Intifada* was still on and the narrow cobbled streets were eerily quiet and virtually empty. It was early afternoon and all the shops and businesses in the covered market streets were closed and locked up behind cold iron doors. I was very wary, as I walked, noticing the young boys skittering about, and waiting at street junctions and behind archways – looking out for the older youths. There were also Israeli soldiers patrolling, in threes and fours; I felt safer with them in sight, but maybe I shouldn't have. Before I left the kibbutz, Alfonso had warned me: 'In the old city, if you hear *Allahu Akba!* Then you know the knife is coming.'

Those boys had a set routine; they wanted to cause distraction by telling a passer by they had dropped something: 'This is for you?' I heard more than once, but I never looked down – always at the shadows in the doorways and behind the pillars and archways, to make eye contact with whoever just happened to be around and let them know I was aware.

I visited the Church of the Holy Sepulchre again, the focus at the centre of the First Crusade's ideals. Even this place was segregated: split into four individually regulated parts, under the care and control of the Roman Catholic, Armenian, Greek Orthodox and Abyssinian, Coptic and Syrian Orthodox priests. I was particularly unimpressed by the little room within the complex, where the monks were selling souvenirs, little crosses of olive wood (they claimed to be from the Garden of Gethsemane), holy water from the Jordan as well as holy earth and holy oil. I saw a grown man break down and cry at one of the Stations of the Cross, but I wasn't feeling it and I left the building soon after.

I saw a lot of the city during the few days I stayed there, lodging in a hostel right off the Via Dolorosa. It was a real old pilgrims' rest, built of cold stone, though I spent little time actually inside the place. It was small and basic, in a way I'd have expected to have been able to experience it a hundred years before – affordable though, and it had attracted an interesting collection of pilgrims from many lands.

I knew I had to visit the Dome of the Rock; that iconic golden domed structure, up on the Temple Mount. It shelters the rock on which Abraham prepared to sacrifice Isaac. It is also the place from where the Prophet Mohamed was lifted during his fabulous 'Night Journey.' The rock was a real boulder, not embellished with brass and silver like in many of the Christian places of worship. I was surprised at how small the building was, in comparison to its importance.

Nearby, almost directly above the Wailing Wall, is the much larger, and in my view, not particularly attractive Al-Aqsa Mosque. I know now that this is the most important Islamic site in Palestine – not the Dome of the Rock, as most people assume – but at the time, I thought the uninspiring shape and dark grey dome on the wide roof structure rather spoilt the view of the mighty Western Wall of King Solomon's Temple. When Jerusalem was taken, during the First Crusade, the Templar Knights stabled their horses inside the mosque: that, along with many other actions by the invading armies of Christendom, still sits as a deep wound in the consciousness of the local Arab population, as well as for those other Muslims world-wide.

The underlying hatred was tangible, and although peaceful Christians were tolerated inside the Arab Quarter of the city, Jews of any category were a definite target. I was re-thinking the wisdom of having allowed Sharon to give me that Army recruit style haircut, which was still short enough to make some people look me over.

There was an Islamic Museum in one part of the mosque complex; it didn't feel to me much like a spiritual environment though. Blood stained garments were displayed on the wall – taken from the eighteen (I think I counted) 'martyrs' who were shot, two years previously, by the IDF inside the compound – I learned they had been stoning Jews who'd come to worship at the Wailing Wall below. This display included photos of the 'martyrs', in life; but I thought that many of the pictures displayed were surely not chosen to show the kinder edge to their characters.

The shops were just opening as I walked back up one of the main streets through the Arab Quarter, and I made the mistake of glancing at a window display. I was immediately commanded to enter the shop, but I declined the request. Then a big, gruff-sounding Arab, on the other side of the street, called out: 'American?' I simply replied 'English' and that was all the opening he needed. 'Welcome!' he said and offered his hand. Once in his grip, he wasn't going to let go and tried to pull me into his lair, demanding I drink tea with him. I had to twist my arm to free myself, saying '*La shokran*' (No thank you) as I walked away positively – this was not a friendly place and neither was the encounter.

I wandered into the stone vaulted *Suq* and was pleased to find everything open for the first time. The narrow empty street was transformed into a lively bazaar full of people, with food and coffee stalls set out. There were racks of clothes, shoes, brassware and various souvenirs on display, and I remember feeling a lot more comfortable with the atmosphere. I was eating some kind of pastry, soaked in warm honey, and drinking hot cinnamon milk; just watching all the frantic business going on around me. All of a sudden, shops started slamming down their hatches and people were locking up. Within the space of five minutes, the place was dead, cold and empty. The *intifada*, as I understood, allowed only strictly adhered to trading windows of opportunity, which pretty much guaranteed a permanently suppressed economy for local businesses.

The atmosphere became cold and threatening too. I was always aware of the possibility of being attacked in the Old City; we had regularly read, in the Jerusalem Post, of Molotov cocktail attacks, as well as stabbings with knives and screwdrivers. My eyes were everywhere ahead of me and I listened for every footfall on the cobbled streets and stone slabs of the step-ways in this maze of crowded buildings and alleyways.

The small diving knife I usually carried in a shoulder bag – along with my maps, guide-book, fruit, biscuits and water bottle – was tucked into the front of my belt, under my denim jacket, as I walked around. The feeling of the quick release scabbard was not an uncomfortable one; it felt like a friend. I wasn't really surprised that the soldiers guarding the way to and from the Temple Mount confiscated it from me. They kept it in the security tunnel, and then gave it back when I returned that way. There was no suggestion of disapproval, that I was carrying a concealed weapon in a public place; it was for my protection, and I clearly had the mute acquiescence of the guardians of the city.

Walking up the Via Dolorosa (Way of Sorrows) to the edge of the Arab Quarter took me to a junction off this main way; really it was the Via Dolorosa that led off to my left and I just carried on straight, into what became the Christian Quarter on the road leading up to the New Gate. I knew that I was virtually the only one on this street, but there were two or three kids playing around up ahead, at the entrance to another road that led off to the right; I suppose they were about fifty yards away and I carried on walking. As I approached the junction, some egg boxes, soaked in fuel, were pushed out alight into my street and then a blue and white Israeli flag came out and landed on the flames. I saw the Star of David burn and melt away from the pyre and stopped where I was.

I couldn't see round the junction, but I was almost at it and didn't want to turn my back to whatever might be happening; I thought I'd rather see the petrol bomb coming from the front than turn away. I stood still – and two little Palestinian girls who had been on the road, some distance behind me, continued up to my position. They looked at me quite strangely, and then the youngest one (about six years old) went over and tried to pull the part burnt flag away from the flames. The boys were gone and the junction was deserted; it was just some burning cardboard and a cheap nylon flag. That scene played on my mind for the rest of the day.

It was Tuesday 22nd December, and I decided to spend the morning in the Jewish quarter, as I'd not been to that part, to see how the comparison was. It was a breath of fresh air – clean and safe, the streets were alive but not overbearing. The Rockefeller Museum was full of archaeological finds from the earliest civilisations in the region and they had uncovered some of the original streets and walls from Roman times and before that even. The old Roman gate and original Cardo (main street) is still there, beneath the more recent cobble streets.

Damascus Gate is the one shown in most of the old post cards and paintings of Jerusalem; it has the interesting crenellations at the top of the wall. The base of the gateway is sunk below the modern street outside the wall and you descend the steps, as if into a culvert, to get into the Old City that way. Immediately inside the gate, the street opens up, giving some space for the food stalls which were open at that time when I went through.

I stood up on the tower ramparts, watching the scanty market scene below me – it had none of the romance depicted in the old pictures and cards. I watched two Arab youths hustling a man who supported himself with a stick; he looked to be at least partially blind and no-one stopped them from tormenting him. What shocked me was that no-one cared, the youths, who'd had their fun, rushed off somewhere else before I could have got down there; I thought I should have shouted out, but I did nothing. The old man continued on his walk and so did I.

I walked along the ramparts as far as the Jaffa Gate at the top of the hill, but couldn't get off there as the access was blocked.

So I turned to retrace my steps and was met by a Jewish family, visiting from Liverpool, who asked me for help. They were scared, and the woman told me that some Arab youths had terrorised her two boys, chasing them along the wall. I was glad I hadn't been able to get off at Jaffa Gate and walked back with this family to the New Gate, where we all got back down to the street.

It was cold and unfriendly out on those streets; I really wanted to like the place, but was struggling to find a justification. The light was going, but I didn't want to be getting back to the hostel so early. I found myself in a Christian tea house, where Christmas music was being played on instruments and there was carol singing too. This was more like it – I've never been religious really, but those old carols, like we sung at school, always got to me. It was like an umbrella of holiness that I could shelter under for a while. I knew them all, and for an hour that evening, I shared tea and cake and Christian goodness with a group of people who had not yet abandoned hope. Then I walked alone, down through the dark covered streets, back to the cold, stone hostel – tomorrow would be another day; a better day perhaps.

I didn't get out until late in the morning; it was raining but some of the shops were open. As I stood in the *Suq*, eating a hot cake for my breakfast, I noticed a little Arab girl standing around right near me. She looked up at me and said 'Hello' and I knew it was the girl in the street from yesterday, when the flag was burning. It was an odd feeling, and as we both smiled, my faith in human nature was instantly restored.

There were two things I still wanted to do before leaving the country: I wanted to see St George's Monastery at Wadi Qelt, and I wanted to be in Bethlehem for Christmas Eve.

I took a bus east towards the Jordan to the turn off for Wadi Qelt, and then walked some way across the Judean Hills to get to this gorge that drains down into the Jericho Plain. The pleasingly-rounded hills were tinged with green and although the sun wasn't out, the rain had at least stopped. There were shepherds out with their small flocks, going about the way they have always done. Looking back west, I could see the edge of the Jerusalem suburbs and down in the Jordan Valley I could make out where Jericho lay.

There was a lot of water in the wadi and I followed it downhill for about an hour; I walked some of the way with a Greek Orthodox priest who was on his way to the little monastery, built into the rock face the far side of the gorge. It was an impressive sight, tucked into a ledge half way up the cliff face, but it wasn't open to the public. The priest pointed out to me a walled up cave in the cliff, above the monastery, where a hermit lived. There was no way up or down to it and the only access of any kind was a basket on a rope; this was for the monks to send food and water up to him.

I made the decision to follow the wadi, on down to Jericho itself; there was a path built along the edge of the ravine and the gorge got deeper and deeper, the further along I walked. I passed several ruins of earlier Christian places along the way and also saw hyrax in the bushes once again. I won't say I wasn't nervous; the further I went from any kind of security, and especially once the valley spread out to reach the outskirts of a town talked about as a no-go area by Israelis and definitely not on the safe list for most travellers.

I knew it was possible to cross the Allenby Bridge into the

Kingdom of Jordan from here – the border guards would allow this as the West Bank was still officially a part of Jordan; you couldn't cross the other way though, it was one-way traffic only.

The water course from the Wadi Qelt had broadened out into a small river and I met a young Palestinian man, about my own age, fording the river and getting his shoes wet. I trusted him, and we walked together into the town. On the way, we came across a sheep with its leg caught on the fence wire. It was rotting where it lay and looked as if it had been there for days. We freed it, but it couldn't stand, so my companion called a boy to fetch a knife from a nearby house. We held the animal's feet while he cut the poor thing's throat, the blood gouting across his hands and draining into the mud.

Tel Jericho is a partially excavated mound, containing the original ancient city which dates back to 8000BC, the oldest walled city in the world. I didn't have time to see much really, given the lateness of the hour, but I did take note that it was a much friendlier place than where I'd come from. It may have had a forbidding reputation, but it was, on the whole, a non threatening atmosphere. I could see a monastery built half way up the Mount of Temptation: the place where Lucifer took Jesus, to show him 'all the Kingdoms of the world' and I would have liked to have looked down from there. I opted for getting the Palestinian bus back up to Jerusalem though, while I knew for sure there was one.

Christmas Eve in the Holy City, and it was raining again. Bethlehem was a high security zone and there was no direct connection. I had to get a bus to a district called Talpiot, where the only buses going in were organised from; the Arab busses weren't running, as the terrorism risk at that time was too high.

There were security checks and a metal-detecting arch, in a building where the IDF controlled the movement of all visitors to Bethlehem over the two main days of the Christmas period. Some effort had been made to welcome Christian pilgrims; Bethlehem-franked postcards, sweets and Jerusalem roses were given out while we waited in the security area to board the buses. People had come from all over the world to be at that place on the day it all began.

The road block was set up just outside the town; that's where everyone had to get off and walk to the wire fences, where another security search was conducted, before we could walk into Manger Square. It was not a festive experience though, more like being channelled through cattle barriers at a livestock market. The first time I had been in Bethlehem, I was free to roam around anywhere inside or out of the town, but on this day the only permitted destination was the Church of the Nativity itself. After another quick search, people were allowed to enter one by one, through the tiny doorway into that massive fortress basilica.

The original archway entrance was still viewable, but had been blocked up, I don't know how long ago, deliberately leaving just a small square entrance allowing people to stoop through in single file. There were no windows below the parapet to soften its façade. The church is not an attractive building from the outside, despite its age and significance; I saw it as just a protective shelter for the Nativity Grotto, and that was where everyone was making for. We filed down the steps to the right of the alter platform that is built on top of the grotto. It was a lovely sight, truly it was; all lit up with candles and the place of the manger was laid with dark red roses.

People were praying in the candlelit cave; there were European nuns, Palestinian Christians, Japanese pilgrims too, as well as this wonderful flourish of colourful robes and hats worn by a group of West Africans. They were obviously three generations of the same family, all decked out in their finest traditional attire. I stayed in the grotto for quite a while, before going back out into the rain in Manger Square.

The atmosphere out there had lost some of its oppressiveness, as no more buses were coming in, and the light was starting to fade too. There was nothing more for me to do other than catch the bus, laid on by the State of Israel, to Jerusalem Central Station and wait for the 405 to Tel Aviv; I would be in plenty of time to collect my stuff from Yaron's place and catch my flight home.

I could see my bus pulling into the station on time, and I stood ready – home and dry, I thought. The very moment it rolled onto the tarmac square, the PA system opened up – in Hebrew and loud! My bus did a U-turn and every other bus at the stops closed doors and evacuated the station, as did the people standing around. I had to ask a soldier, on the platform, what was going on and he confirmed that it was a bomb alert: 'Everyone must leave the station immediately, so let's get the fuck out of here.'

I don't know where my bus went to, but it wasn't coming back, so we went along the road to a spot where the IDF hitches for rides – you see them hitching everywhere and they always get picked up quickly. It's a good system, as the army needs to be spread out everywhere to protect the population – all the time.

I got a lift into Tel Aviv and made it to Yaron's place in time.

He was a bus driver himself, but also an army reservist; he told me that the previous week he had been on patrol in the north and his team 'caught some terrorists' infiltrating the border from Lebanon. It was in the area where I had been the week before. Yaron's intensity stepped up, as he told me it was night time and he had been the first to make contact: bringing the prisoners in without a shot fired.

Yaron was no xenophobe, despite having grown up in Iran before the revolution. When we were in the Darien, I remember him telling me about a time in New York's Central Park, when he'd noticed a Middle Eastern family having a picnic and he'd recognised that they were speaking Persian, so he stopped to say hello. Yaron said they'd been really friendly and welcoming and had asked him to share their picnic with them. The conversation had been about Iran before the Ayatollah and how good everything had been, but the moment he'd said: 'and now I live in Israel.' they'd shut up instantly, pulled their children to their feet and left him standing there.

My final hurdle was the airport itself. I hadn't really thought about all the extra security implications of flying home from Israel on Christmas Eve to be honest; I'd thought it would be quite a nice experience. After a two hour baggage search, I was swearing I'd never do that again. I don't blame them, they were nice enough about it and I think they found it quite funny, going through all the weird and wonderful junk I was carrying.

They pulled out every single thing and some of it, like my NBC (nuclear, biological and chemical) suit, which was sealed up to preserve its lifespan, had to be taken off to be individually ex-rayed. Of course I had a gas mask, a folding shovel, a diver's knife, army water bottles and stuff like that. Then there were the two half-inch thick, glass discs I had swiped from *Aram* – to use on a diving boat I was planning to build. There was stuff I'd picked up at the kibbutz dump too: slices of a hardwood tree we'd felled. I had containers of Saharan sand and a little glass bottle of sandalwood oil from Egypt. I had two small bottles of olive oil, which had been pressed from olives collected from the trees in the kibbutz garden as well as a whole roll of Clingfilm.

This was all an amusing curiosity for the young soldiers who were going through it, but they got funny about my army coat, saying it was IDF property and I shouldn't have it. I'm not sure they believed me when I said I'd found it, abandoned amongst the old wool and muck in one of the sheep pens. That was a fact, and no-one was going to claim it, so I'd washed it out and found it to be quite serviceable; true, I hadn't asked permission, but there hadn't been a problem with me keeping it. The blue shirts and shorts (standard work-wear on any kibbutz) I'd decided to take with me as souvenirs spoke for themselves. I had worked for food and drink at that place and got quite attached to the stuff I'd worn day in and day out. I thought it was fair enough and the security detail just tutted and shook their heads as a reprimand.

That security team got finished with me at 02:15 and my plane was scheduled to fly at 02:20; I hadn't even checked in and thought I'd surely missed it. But my new best friends rushed me through to the gate with a boarding pass they'd ordered up for me, and in a way that helped out. My baggage weighed close to fifty kilos and I hadn't considered the weight restrictions at all. There was no time for any of that: they took my two packs to the plane and I ran along with a bulging shoulder bag, sweating but relieved.

I cherish the memories I have of my time in Israel, and I still have that old army coat they let me keep. I also kept various cards and aerogramme letters that had been sent to me whilst there, as well as those sent to me by fellow volunteers after I'd left. Reading through these recently, I was amused by the simplistic juvenility we must have all shared during our times there, and thought a transcript from Michelle's January update deserved a place at the end of this chapter:

Life here is same as usual. I've got a day off, Karen is off sick and Tony is off 'cos he put a knife through his leg while making a cricket bat!!!

So we've just had a game of Risk and I'm making a board for trivial pursuit. Xmas and New Year were a good laugh; everything went okay in the end. Risk was banned for two weeks, Alfonso got pissed as expected, Karen and Tony kept us amused with their constant arguments and Barbara spends most of her time away from us. Stein and Holly are still lovey-dovey while Jens is in love with a new South African volunteer who turned up with another Canadian girl; she lasted three hours and got the next bus out. I don't think this new girl will last long either though – she told them she only wanted to work in the garden or sheep – at the moment she's in the kitchen permanently.

Good news was none of us had aids and I'm leaving the kibbutz on 2nd Feb. I'm probably going to Egypt for two weeks then home.*

Gaston – one of the new Dutch volunteers is a first class cretin. He's still in the Jimi Hendrix era, looks like a hippy and is always strumming away on his guitar and writing songs. His latest is called 'The Kibbutz Song' This is how it goes: 'This is the kibbutz song' (repeat 50 times).

We went to Jerusalem yesterday, just for the day. It was really good – better than the last trip. Gabi came with us so the food was much better (naturally). We went to all the usual tourist places. Gaston got chucked out of the church 'cos he lit up a cigarette (moron)!!! A greasy Arab came up to me and said I remind him of Samantha Fox (wanker). Rest of the day was spent looking at old ruins and listening to our tour guide go on and on and on etc.

*[The HIV tests were a requirement of the Kibbutz Movement medical department and we all got tested just before I left; they sent my results home to the UK.]

I did meet Tony, Karen and Michelle – about four years later – in Jersey, where they were all working in hotels. We laughed half the night away, about all the silly stuff that had happened when we were volunteers.

Just prior to my original trip to Egypt, I had bought a copy of the popular English language newspaper, The Jerusalem Post. I kept that paper as a souvenir; it was dated Sunday December 17th 1989. Reading through this time capsule (in faded print) that had been at the bottom of a box in my loft for twenty-nine years, I can see why I saved it. Along with headlines like: *Cairo car bomb, Hezbollah terrorist alert for West Europe and Black Panther movement returns to Nablus*, a portion of the front page contained an article entitled: *USSR vows to slash military spending*. The article stated that the Kremlin had pledged to bring home more than 600,000 troops stationed in foreign countries, by the turn of the century – well they came home a lot quicker than that!

Inside the eight page broadsheet, key articles included *Austria to pay social benefits to Nazi victims, Haifa expected to absorb massive influx of Soviet Jews* and *Jews foresee "Great danger" at the prospect of unification of the two Germanys*. There was also some lesser news about Jewish and Arab academies demonstrating side-by-side for the re-opening of the Palestinian universities in the occupied territories and also about a fight at the Western Wall, because of a disagreement over interpretations of the Torah, where Yeshiva students had attacked the publisher of the Torah Outreach Program with a chair. Ya'acov Fogelman had apparently called out for help to nearby soldiers – who told him that stopping fights among Jews was not their job.

The last article was about a PLO-Syrian gunfight erupting near Sidon in Lebanon where fourteen were killed and forty wounded. Lebanon was most certainly a basket case – the playground of the armies of Syria and Israel, as well as a free for all between the factions of Iran's Hezbollah (Shiites in the Bekaa Valley) and Arafat's Fatah (Sunni Islamists), the ruling party in the Palestine Liberation Organization during the nineties – the growing pots for this, being the UN monitored refugee camps in Jordan and Lebanon.

During the eighties, Lebanon had hit the headlines with the Israeli invasion, and then the massacre of thousands of Palestinian refugees, by the Christian Phalange militia outside Beirut. There were several high-publicity kidnappings of Westerners too, including that of Church of England envoy Terry Waite: chained up to a radiator in a dark basement for four years. I wasn't even aware Lebanon had a government, let alone an army of its own and whatever was up there, everyone knew it wasn't a place they wanted to go.

The nineties went on for Israel, with various key figures in the headlines: Yitzhak Rabin, Shimon Perez, Yasser Arafat and Ariel Sharon come instantly to mind, but 1992 spelled the end of my involvement in the Levant and I would not see the Middle East again for another thirteen years.

PART THREE

The essence of Arabia

CHAPTER THIRTEEN: Eastern promises

After the Second Gulf War had been decided, and a whole new phase of endless conflict emerged from the ashes of Saddam Hussein's pleasure garden, I thought I'd like to see what all this oil wealth actually meant for the various states along the Persian Gulf – I wanted to see it before that was gone too.

Dubai, in 2005, was quite a shock for me really. I was only there for a few days and nights on a flight stop-over, before continuing on to the Far East. I wanted to see tradition and culture in an Arab land untouched by trouble and war; how decadent could eastern promise be?

My hotel was named the St. George, and it was in a district called Deira, right by the creek, which is the main tidal inlet. All the big wooden, ocean-going dhows were moored there, and always have been. There they were, ready to sail the ancient trade routes: to the Indian subcontinent and all down the east coast of Africa, as far as the island of Zanzibar – that place which had made its wealth from the slave trade, a thousand years before Britain ever transported *negros* from the River Gambia to the American colonies.

I arrived after dark, by taxi, but my driver was not an Arab. Menial work in the Gulf States is the reserve of the migrant underclass, and taxi drivers are mostly Indian men. The authorities are strict on migrant labour and the foreigners have to leave their wives (or husbands) and children behind, for very long contracted periods. I found this interesting but also disappointing; not that all the good jobs were reserved for the state's own citizens, but because it was thus rare to meet one of these indigenous Arab citizens of a Gulf State, during any regular day to day encounter at least.

There were the Filipinos and Thais, of course, who ran the St. George, which was a basic, low impression hotel, and had a restaurant I couldn't use. I had arrived during *Ramadan*, which meant I could only select food items from a restricted list on the menu. Food would then be brought to my room for me. Well that didn't seem like much of an experience, so I went to sample the atmosphere of the hotel bar. Foreigners only – were allowed to drink alcohol, but at very high prices – and I would have been able to, if it hadn't been *Ramadan*.

I went up to the bar and bought a Turkish coffee, then looked around for a place to sit. There was soft music playing, the lighting was low and the floor was dotted with small tables that would fit couples or single patrons only. They were spaced out so that each couple could be afforded some privacy in their conversations, but there were no couples; single ladies sat at most of them, keeping a discrete eye on the few male customers in the room, while pretending to sip their fruit juices.

Of course I looked at them, there was nothing else to do and I'd never seen Arab taxi-girls before. I was curious to see how the procedure was conducted and it seemed to be that the few Arab men, who sat at their own tables by the walls, spent a long time leering intensely at the women. The lady would occasionally, by a motion of her eyes, invite a customer to sit at her table. A short conversation would follow, but without any physical or emotional connection; then the man would generally return to his stake-out table to consider his options.

Most of the women there were quite full of form, as much as their conservative clothing would allow the eye to judge, but I caught the eye of one slim, and slightly androgynous looking lady, sporting heavy mascara. On her third attempt I thought: 'What the hell' and went over to see what kind of a conversation I could have. At close quarters, this mysterious beauty was far from bursting with eastern promise; there was no small talk and not even any friendliness, it was straight down to the mathematics of time for money. Her technique was awful – she only bothered to smile about twice – and the one single discussion subject permissible was based around how many hundreds of US dollars it would cost me to strike up a relatively short relationship, albeit based on mutual respect for religious tolerance, the laws of the land and my own expected generosity. It was a short conversation – then she turned her eyes off, just as if flipping a venetian blind.

I bought another Turkish coffee from the Thai barman and then ambled on up to my room to watch TV alone.

It was early afternoon, and I was out in a Toyota Land Cruiser with a Canadian couple and a pair of Japanese girls. Our flamboyant Pakistani driver was sporting an Arab *shemagh* head cloth and we were all going out to the desert sands.

The dunes were quite a bit further out than I'd imagined, but the cost (per head) for the trip was affordable and I had to see the sands of Arabia. We weren't the only group out there that day; there were six or eight other 4x4 vehicles we teamed up with before the fun began, and the last road we crossed was more like a final barrier between the built-up city and the endless sea of yellow. Some of the sand had made its way across the road to the petrol station where we stopped to prep the vehicle, by letting out more than half of the air from our tyres to stop us bogging down in the dunes out there.

It was a good day and the Jap' girls couldn't stop screaming in the back, it was so funny. I was amazed at the angles and degrees we were able to take without digging in and flipping, the driver was pretty good and he was really throwing us into it. I was impressed by the capabilities of the modern Toyota Land Cruisers, although I still didn't like the jelly mould shape.

The sun got low in the sky, almost without warning, and we were driving in a convoy along the ridge of a dune, chasing the red orb. No sooner had it disappeared into the sandy grey yonder than we came upon the Bedouin camp we were to spend the evening at. It was in a sheltered hollow, like the form of a frying pan and we'd approached it along the pan handle. There was simple food laid out in a buffet and lots of hot, sweet tea, as much as we wanted. Some traditional music was playing, but we missed out on the dancers – we were told they wouldn't perform during *Ramadan* – so that was that.

It was still a good atmosphere despite any disappointment, we got a ride on a camel, and then dined on dates and yogurt, flatbread and chopped fresh tomatoes and cucumber. The group I was in all got on fine and the only irritating character was the Pakistani driver, who was trying just a little too hard.

I'm sure there are all sorts of great things to do in Dubai, but I only had time and money for one desert visit, a look around the boats on the creek the next day and a trip to the other side of the water. This was where the real life was going on, in the old narrow streets that led between markets and mosques, and eventually to the eighteenth century fort that looked like it was made from blocks of dried sand. The United Arab Emirates was only formed in 1971 and the Al-Fahidi Fort, which doubles as the city museum, is the oldest building in Dubai still standing.

It was the traditional architecture and the activity of the true locals that I found on that other side of the creek, which made me want to visit all the other Gulf states in turn. It was neat and tidy, but proper and real; that was what I had hoped to see – not the dusty, characterless streets behind the St. George that sported building rubble, plastic bags and flies. Everyone knows about the tall buildings in Dubai and the man-made islands, created off-shore out in the pristine waters for millionaires to own. It didn't bother me that I hadn't been out there to see all that before I left. It's the view from the air that makes it anyway, and I'll bet the sea wasn't as clean as it had been before they messed around with nature.

So that was my first experience of Arabian sands, and it was a good start, aside from an enlightening chance meeting with a group of three or four Iranian tourists on that first night. They were clearly on a controlled budget, and had no shame in telling me that they were all sharing an apartment in a part-developed district out by the airport. Their room wasn't the only thing they were clubbing together on either. They were there for the Syrian and Lebanese women that sit in those coffee bars. The UAE is well known as the hedonistic centre of the Middle East; they may pray piously, five times a day, back home in their restrictive Islamic states, but they can't find whiskey and freelance hookers in their own coffee shops, I'm guessing.

My next attempt at getting to know the region took me to Qatar, in 2007. The experience was a little disappointing and no match for Dubai; being a low-lying protrusion off the shores of Saudi Arabia's east coast, the landscape was uninspiring. It was okay, but difficult to find any kind of true culture. Qatar has oil and nothing much else. The city of Doha was not particularly interesting in any way, and had nothing really to appeal to my sense of romantic adventure. It was expensive to be there and all the shops and services I came into contact with were run by either Indians or Bangladeshis.

I paid a taxi driver to take me about fifteen kilometres south, to a place called Awakra Beach, which is in a wide crescent of stony shore-land that shelters the traditional fishing fleet. It was vaguely interesting and might have carried some atmosphere too, if the beach hadn't been strew with old building rubble. The shallow, flat-calm water held a layer of still air over it that was laced with diesel fumes, so it wasn't pleasant swimming. Once out there, I noticed the occasional froth of floating excrement that must have drifted out from where the fishing boats were moored.

The Pearl Qatar was still under construction, so the amazing, futuristic, luxury complex advertised on the tourist maps could be viewed from the outside only. It wasn't much of a detour, and I had time to kill, after the one nearby fort I'd spotted on the map turned out to be empty and out of bounds; it wasn't pretty either. If my taxi hadn't passed by a horse racing stables, right beside the main road on the way back into town, then I would never have seen the racing camels also kept there. They were big and handsomely formed, kept in a condition to shame the whole of Egypt. Those beasts were properly fed, groomed and exercised – no trudging sullenly about under the burden of a day's fruitless labour.

If the taxi drivers were Indians, the hotels staff Thais and the construction workers from Pakistan and Bangladesh, then the nannies and maids were Indonesians and Filipinas. It happened that I was sitting next to one on the plane, a woman in a headscarf from the southern Philippine island of Mindanao. She was on her way home to her family, after completing a contracted period for a rich Arab family. She told me she hated her employers, as they always shouted at her and mistreated her; even the kids got to have a go. I had thought that, being fellow Muslims, the culture would have afforded these women, far from home, some kind of respect and protection. This woman was adamant: 'They are all bastards' she told me through gritted teeth.

CHAPTER FOURTEEN:
Snow in the desert

Since my first journey to the crusade lands, traversing the lengths and breadths of Israel and Egypt, I'd harboured a desire to cross the Jordan River to the Hashemite Kingdom of the same name. I wanted to see the wonders of Petra, to explore Wadi Rum and to look back across the Red Sea at the Gulf of Aqaba. I wanted to see Israel from the other side – the West Bank had only been a territory under that name since Jordan annexed it in 1950, and then it came into Israeli hands in 1967 – I wondered how different the eastern bank could be.

The visa on arrival was a simple affair of ten Jordanian dinars; there were no questions and not even a form to fill out. I had only five full days to see what I could, so I booked a taxi tour from the hotel to get me going for day one.

My man was a young Palestinian refugee who'd been born in Kuwait to parents who had fled the Israeli occupation, but had not been welcomed into Jordan itself. It seemed that the Palestinians, although championed by all of the region and encouraged to fight against Israel, were not popular guests amongst Israel's neighbours. Egypt didn't want Gazans and Jordan didn't want Palestinians. In fact it was only after Lawrence of Arabia united the Bedouin tribes to help drive out the Turks, that the old crusader territory of Outré-Jordain was able to grow into a nation: at first named Transjordan, it had always been an important trade route between Constantinople and the Gulf of Aqaba. Mohammed (my driver) seemed nice enough, though I decided not to mention that I'd lived in Israel.

Amman was cold (I reckoned about four to six degrees) and a fog covered most of it; it was late winter but I hadn't been expecting it to be quite as harsh. I wanted to view the Dead Sea from Mount Nebo, which was the promontory where Moses is said to have stood when he beheld the Promised Land. I could see the northern edge of the Dead Sea from this place and the Plain of Moab, stretching out to the Palestinian city of Jericho and the Judean Hills.

We drove down the winding road into the rift valley, leaving the fog up there behind us. The air became warmer and it was pleasant, but certainly not hot. When we got to the shore we found that the water was quite choppy and I didn't fancy a splash in the face from that searing mineral solution, so I just squatted by the edge and put my hand in. I tasted the water, as I had back in 1989 and sure enough, it was offensively bitter. From this position by the lake bed I could see Qumran, where the Dead Sea Scrolls had been found. Nebo was easily made out, jutting out proud from the escarpment.

Mohammed told me that before his family had fled Kuwait, during the Iraqi invasion of 1990, he had been used to swimming every day in the warm blue water of the Persian Gulf. He said when he found himself in Jordan, he had come down to the evaporating mineral water here and plunged in, then staggered out in a blind panic from the pain it was causing to his eyes and nasal passages. We laughed together, he was honest and non-condescending and I started to trust him to be my guide.

The Jordan River, when it leaves the Kinneret in Galilee, is wide and deep enough to swim in. It flows down to the Dead Sea and the sun does the rest. But twenty years previously, it was still a river when it got to Jericho. Unfortunately, and mostly due to Israel taking the water for their irrigation needs, by the time the flow gets past Jericho it is now merely a wide swampy stream, and the most famous of the world's inland seas is drying up at an alarming rate – it will soon be gone.

In 1999, archaeologists were able to uncover what has been identified as the site where Jesus was baptised: the place is called Bethany-beyond-the-Jordan, and is in the area where it's believed John-the-Baptist lived as a hermit, on a diet of honey and locusts.

Byzantine monuments and facilities for pilgrims have been uncovered from the silt of a thousand years at this newest of biblical sites, on a little bend in the ancient water course, where the sluggish flow is a caramel-brown colour and surrounded by tall rushes and scrubby trees.

The border with Israel was just metres away in the middle of the stream and I descended the stone steps to be there. A giant stone font, many centuries old, was still there at the edge; the mud dredged out of it, to be accessible once more for religious services. However, right there opposite, and rising from the other bank, was a brand new set of white limestone steps in Roman imperial style, that led down from the new Israeli-built visitor centre. There were no fences or guards, which amazed me more than the archaeological revelation itself.

If it were still 1990, there would have been soldiers on either side, primed to shoot anyone getting close to that same piece of water. But the two governments had signed the peace treaty in

1994 that had opened up the borders for their mutual benefit; I don't know if Jordan *really* gave up its intentions regarding the West Bank, but officially sited immigration points do make a reality of it. Two years after Israel's Prime Minister, Yitzhak Rabin, shook hands with Yasser Arafat on the White House lawn, he was assassinated by a Jewish zealot and Israel got the hardliner government that they didn't all necessarily want. King Hussein of Jordan died of natural causes in 1999. Arafat died in 2004 of 'a mystery blood disorder' (the official statement): speculations have included the possibility of assassination by poison – other suggestions are cirrhosis, AIDS, or even simple food poisoning.

Back at the (three star) Hotel Toledo, I thought I would use the gymnasium. It was in the basement, but when I found it I was disappointed, and not just because the sign on the door stated: MEN ONLY. The air was stale and the equipment all sticky, there was a swimming pool, jacuzzi and steam-room attached to the gym though; I looked in and thought better of it.

I was down there already, so I just used some of the free weights for a bit, but I wasn't into it; there were sweaty men in unattractive vest tops, who were obviously regular users, and the facility probably was of a standard one should expect at the lower end of the scale. What really amused me was seeing a fully robed and bearded middle-aged Arab come in, sporting the addition of some cheap tracksuit trousers. He did take his headdress off, but not the robe which couldn't hide his obvious paunch. I watched him play on the elliptical, high-stride machine for a while and it was hilarious.

I booked Mohammed as my driver for the next three days,

from the hotel travel kiosk, I liked him. I didn't like his boss, who was a slimy conniving lizard, who didn't even try to hide his guile as he briefed Mohammed intensely – you don't need to follow the language to know when a scheme is being discussed right in front of you – Mohammed looked uncomfortable under the grilling he was getting, but I knew he needed that job and I also knew it was his responsibility, during the coming three days, to fleece me of all the money he thought I might have. Mohammed would claim his cut from the boss at the end, but he wasn't in control and I knew that.

The King's Highway goes south all the way to the sea, with various points to branch off at along the way, and the first stop was Kerak. The enormous castle was built on a savagely steep hillside promontory, with the modern town attached outside the walls of the gatehouse. Originally built by crusaders, then rebuilt by Mamluk Turks, it's a huge site: a semi-ruined top level, with a warren of tunnels and steps and underground vaulted galleries. I spent about two hours there but I could have spent all day.

We stopped for lunch in the town outside the walls and I wanted to change money; the money changers were right there amongst the small shops, cafés and hostels. The man who I dealt with in his own shop had naturally ginger hair and freckles; I had seen this in more than one Palestinian face on the streets of Jerusalem years before. This man in Kerak, with Arab features and a Northern-European complexion was not the only one in the town with that genetic peculiarity, and I came to the conclusion that, as this town originated as a result of the castle being built, there would have been plenty of mixing going on during the hundred years of European occupation there.

We continued south across the rolling hills and there was almost nothing to look at on the eastern side of the road; it flattened out into a stony grey waste that Mohammed said went all the way to the Persian Gulf.

We turned off shortly, to our right, and headed a little way towards the rift where the hills were smooth-looking and covered in clean, white, broken stones. This was shepherding land and we saw the occasional flock grazing on the scant pale hill-grass. The shepherd children in this region guard and guide the flocks, using the stones at their feet to throw to either side of any wayward animal, to make it move in the desired direction.

The very first outpost of the crusader satellite state of Outré-Jordain had been a small circular stone castle, built on a conical hill and named Montréal – now referred to locally as *Shoubak*. From there the knights could set out to control the transit of trade caravans. Montréal is ruined, isolated and abandoned; we were the only people there, except for a few Arab workers engaged (very casually) in some restoration work.

It was bright and clear, but still cold, and I was much amused to see that the workers had gathered enough residual snow to build a small pillar of it into the form of an Arab man in a makeshift *shemagh* they'd fashioned from red and white safety barrier tape. There had been a village, I could see, further down the slope on the side of the next hill, which was probably abandoned around the time the outpost had become obsolete. I liked this place.

We passed more piles of snow by the roadside, as we continued on our route south; the hills had a light dusting of it, which made it hard to see what was loose stone and what was actually snow.

Petra is an ancient city of carved stone, founded by the Nabataeans. It is sited on lower ground, where the rift valley breaks up into canyons of stone, much darker than the hills we'd been travelling through so far. This was the north/south divide and it's the same as on the other side of the border – you hit a ridge in the 'Bible Lands' around about the level of Beersheba, and then you realise you are no longer in the land of 'Milk and Honey' – it's warmer all of a sudden, and dryer; geologically you are already in North Africa.

Mohammed gave me two hours and twenty minutes, which wasn't long enough, but we needed to reach Wadi Rum by sunset. I didn't realise that, although he had been there before, he'd only ever walked through the *Siq* – that narrow passage that Harrison Ford and Sean Connery galloped their horses through in the film *Indiana Jones and the Last Crusade* – it's really a crack in the rock mass, about half a mile long, with towering cliffs either side, which led me directly to the huge monument referred to as the Treasury or Al-Khazneh. Carved out of a sheer, rose-pink cliff-face of gloriously-marbled rock, it was an awesome sight – despite the crowds getting in my way, walking slowly in silly tourist hats, or riding donkeys slowly.

I found Petra to be the only place in Jordan that had become so famous that it wasn't a pleasure to be there, and despite all of the contained wonder of the place, it almost felt as if a part of Egypt had arrived just to show the local hawkers how it's done. Yes, it was that kind of hustle, but not really persistent enough to be offensive, just that there were so many of them that I couldn't appreciate what an amazing place I was walking through – so I just kept walking.

The whole site is miles wide, once you get into it, and you could hike for a couple of days through the various canyons and the trails to the high places if you chose. I walked briskly through the tight mass of people, as the main canyon opened out into a wide space, with monuments on either side, carved into solid rock; all pink, brown and beige hues. I carried on walking, up and out from the valley floor, on my way to reach the Monastery of Ad-Deir, right up high on its own isolated plateau.

The wide pathway became a narrow trail as it started to climb the escarpment, leaving the big groups down below. I was overtaking as I went, but as it was mid-afternoon, most of the people in my way were coming down already and I soon found I had the rock-cut stairways almost to myself. I found I'd left all the hawkers, donkey-men and self appointed guides behind me as I'd forced the pace onwards and the steps had become too narrow.

It took me quite a while to get up onto the massif where Ad-Deir sits, carved in deep relief, out of pale caramel coloured sandstone. The views were fantastic and there were hardly any visitors still up there. The sun carried a pleasant kind of warmth and the air was cool.

I picked a viewing spot at the edge of the cliff to the south-west, where the massif drops away into other canyons, before opening up to form Wadi Araba: a wide empty valley that only ends when it reaches the waters of the Gulf of Aqaba.

I really liked this high place, but couldn't stay long because of the time it would take me to get back to the car. The heels of my cheap desert boots were disintegrating too, and I thought I would be lucky to get back down with the soles still attached.

I was half an hour late getting back to where Mohammed was waiting with the car – and so we had to get a move on, and get across the next set of high hills before the light faded out – it was four o'clock and sunset was supposed to be about five-thirty.

These next hills were sprinkled with snow too. I'd thought we would have left all that behind, but we had to stop on the last high stretch of the road, before plunging down into the flat, sandy desert. The sight was almost unfathomable: a family, by the side of the road, was just putting the finishing touches to a pretty good snowman they had made. Actually there were three or four cars stopped, in the space of a mile, all with local families out there building snowmen. It wasn't that cold, I didn't think, but they all had hats and scarves on and we had real snow in the desert.

The road dropped down a thousand metres – was my guess – onto the red desert floor of the Wadi Rum expanse. The sun was just setting and the mesa-type (table-toped) mountains that rose up out of the sand seemed to glow. Mohammed drove me to a Bedouin camp-site – there were two or three of these – established to give tourists the desert experience. It wasn't cheap at forty Jordanian dinars – that was not far-off fifty quid – for a bed in a long black goat-hair tent, with dinner and breakfast thrown in. There was a youth group staying there at the site when I arrived, from an 'American International' school in Cairo, and the buffet dinner was already out on the tables.

There was some music and singing – pretty non-descript was what I wrote in my journal – but the food was okay and the camp-site was nice enough, with unlimited helpings of sweet tea.

After dinner, I went for a walk across the stiff flat stretch of packed sand, to get me to some of the rock formations. It was quite an eerie experience, passing between these horsts of rock; even if it wasn't completely silent, due to the two active camp-sites nearby, and the occasional pick-up truck crossing one way or another, the outcrops of rock cut the noise out very effectively.

I saw my way by the light of the stars and a crescent moon – it was like being on a boat with a calm sea – just how I'd remembered seeing the heavens all those years before, when I'd first come to the Middle-East and everything was like a picture book.

I ascended a steep bank of soft, pale sand, driven by winds up the side of a rock I'd just passed behind; it led me to a bit of a saddle on the top and it was steep and hard going. I was careful to keep away from odd lumps of rock and their shadows, as best I could, in case I disturbed any snakes or scorpions. I could see the lights of our camp from my position on top and it was nice to sit up there, completely alone and absorbing as much solitude as the soul demanded. It was a nice temperature too, and not a breath of wind.

My rock was at least a hundred feet high, but in the strange light I couldn't make out where the edges dropped off to the desert floor below, or where the sand graded up to meet them, close enough to reach. I decided to be safe and go back down the way I'd come.

Once back at the camp, things were quietening down and I took some more tea before retiring to my shelter for the night. It wasn't a comfortable night really, I was bitten a fair few times, on the face and hands, by tiny mosquitoes, before I adopted the old method of sleeping – in a wide-brimmed hat, supporting a cotton scarf draped from brim to chin and keeping hands beneath the covers – I was pleased it was not a humid night, the goat-hair tent material kept the chill out of my sleeping quarters and I got by.

I woke at dawn and was out of the compound by first light and up on top of a different rock. It was smoothly rounded, this one, and quite odd. It felt as if I was the size of an ant and climbing up onto a massive irregular pebble. It was more difficult than I had expected, and cold up there too, but I was safely on top by sunrise and could see the whole panorama, with the sun lighting the rocks pink. I remembered that punishing night I'd spent on Mount Moses in the Sinai, and what a relief it had been to see the sky become light and to feel those first rays of warmth, as the sun had emerged from the Arabian Mountains.

I found it quite difficult to identify the safe way down from that globular mound. It was like descending a three-headed loaf of bread which was a lot higher than it had looked from the ground. I headed straight for the camp and took some tea beside the fire and waited for the buffet breakfast to be spread out.

Wadi Rum was the main pilgrimage route to Mecca, before oil and aeroplanes made it all too easy. I can see the spiritualism in a journey a month long, it's why we climb mountains – to get through an ordeal and clear the mind for some higher inspiration. The wadi is a natural route, passing between high and inhospitable mountains and barren empty desert. The Bedouin know there is water here though, under the sand, and it's where Lawrence of Arabia waited to meet the Arab tribal leaders, before directing them to attack the Turks at Aqaba.

A larger-than-life Bedouin driver called Abdulla Karem took me by Land Cruiser pick-up to see some of the places of interest that lay nearby. I was shown a canyon with pictorial inscriptions on the rock-face, done thousands of years ago, my guide told me, by the Nabataeans. There were images of men hunting, on foot and from the backs of camels. Other pictures were of lions, ostriches and other birds and animals that once inhabited the area. These scrawlings looked prehistoric, and were clear evidence of a time before the desert had stripped the landscape of its life.

Before we returned to the camp I was brought to a small tent set-up, to take tea with a family out there. It was interesting, but also hinted that the simple and timeless way of living was being intruded upon – and not by me either. It was the mobile phone that a father and son were sharing with interest; they were watching YouTube videos of Arab women jiggling around in low cut tops, or just in their big, unattractive underwear. The older male grinned at me like a hyena and simply said 'Syria.' Meanwhile, the women in the camp got on with their work, consciously ensuring that their faces could not be looked upon by any visitors; it was just Abdulla and me, the younger girls went and hid in another tent.

During those few days on the road with Mohammed, we talked a lot and he told me how things were, in more ways than one, for young Arab men. Apparently, men from Amman regularly made trips across the northern border: sometimes to Damascus, but often just to the first town along the road. This was a few years before 'the Arab Spring' and I was quite shocked to hear that Syria was then a dirty word to Jordanians and if your friends and family knew you were going there, they just thought it was for sexual adventures with prostitutes. Jordanian men going there, for whatever reason, would routinely make up a lie to explain their absence, perhaps stating that they were staying with relatives somewhere else.

Mohammed also told me that amongst the Palestinian community – that being one of the most liberal-minded Arab societies – it was not impossible for a girl and a boy to be in a pre-marital relationship. This did however require so much commitment to keep the girl's family accepting of the situation that the whole thing would wear a young man down, often driving him to somewhat less salubrious encounters elsewhere. Mohammed told me he did have a girlfriend, but he didn't want to marry just yet; he said he loved spending time on the road away from her, as she was often jealous and clinging, but he didn't want to break-up and cause a family fall-out.

I did get around to asking how Mohammed felt about Israel and he said he had never been to Palestine. When he was forced to leave Kuwait he had spent a lot of time praying, but he hardly ever prayed these days and now he didn't even hate the Israelis. Jordan wouldn't make him a citizen, as the government didn't want to absorb a landless people; despite the fact the Kingdom had lost the land in the West Bank as a direct result of their own offensive in the Six Day War. Mohammed just wanted to live his life, and it seemed to me that he was enjoying things.

Aqaba, the port town and gateway to the Red Sea was very understated, compared to Eilat with its neat white block buildings clear to see, just a couple of miles along the beach. All the buildings on the Jordanian side seemed to be sand-coloured, with the only high-rise ones being the three or so top-name, luxury hotels that commandeered all of the accessible beach space as part of their private resorts. Locals and regular visitors alike, now have to drive five miles towards the Saudi border to find a public beach to swim from. We did just that, and found it to be dirty and a bit gravely, it was a major disappointment.

There was as much cigarette waste and broken glass as there was genuine sand. But the sea looked as I'd remembered it: a thin pale-blue strip along the edge, then that deep indigo-blue as it plunges down to frightening depths. The base of the mountains, at this point, started right by the shore and they were notably taller than the ones five or ten kilometres over on the other side of the gulf.

I was shocked to find the sea was cold, there was a breeze and it was choppy too. The sun was warm, but the air cool. I'd swum from Eilat in January before and the temperature had been fine, but this was March and I was shivering in the water! I could see where the road led from Eilat to Taba and the Egyptian border and remembered that I had walked that distance once and my lips had cracked in the hot dry breeze.

When we'd stopped outside the hotel Mohammed took me to, before checking in, he contacted his boss using his mobile phone and it sounded like he was getting a telling off. Mohammed then said I should give him the money to pay for my room and he would do the deal at the reception desk while I stayed in the car; the reason he gave was so that I wouldn't be overcharged. I smelt a rat okay, but I went along with it and waited to be called in to do the passport registration without seeing any money changing hands. A little bit of discrete investigation later and I identified that I'd been overcharged by about five JDs. I know Mohammed felt guilty about it

– although I never let on that I knew – because when we went out to eat at a restaurant later, I prepared to pay our bill and he seemed to be genuinely offended and protested that he was able to pay for his own meal.

The drive back to Amman the next day was only three and a half hours, but we didn't get back until after dark. I had to keep Mohammed talking for the last hour, as he'd fallen asleep at the wheel three times!

The plan was for me to take a day off and explore the city a bit and then we would reconvene the following day for the drive up to the north. I found it to be a larger city than I had at first realised. The hill on which the remains of the Amman Citadel stand has been occupied since Neolithic times and has the remains of all expanding cultures in the region since; it also houses the Museum of the Dead Sea Scrolls. I hadn't realised that the majority of the scrolls were here and not in Jerusalem.

Umm Qais (Gadara) is a Roman era ruin on a hilltop overlooking the Galilee. I so much wished to look down over the places where I'd roamed as a young back-packing traveller and wayward kibbutz volunteer. Tiberias on the lake was clearly visible and I thought I could identify the Horns of Hattin up above and beyond. I could see the snow-covered top of Mount Hermon, above a haze surrounding the Golan Heights. I could make out Mount Tabor, where I'd spent that night on the eve of Yom Kippur, and Nazareth, where I'd visited on the same day I was attacked by the viper. Belvoir, on its hilltop promontory, was there in front of me, just the other side of the valley and I remembered the hike to get up there and the heat of that day.

It was early springtime in the Holy Land and the hills were sheathed in a gentle green. Many little white flowers (like daisies) and red ones (like poppies) speckled the ground under the olive groves that led down the slope towards the Yarmouk River Gorge, where, years ago, the bus had driven along to get us to Hamat Gader.

All the defensive trenches and pill-boxes that had been manned on this side before the peace deal were empty and in disrepair, they were silting up with loose soil and had been used as rubbish pits. I did see two soldiers observing the valley down below, but clearly no one was expecting war to break out in the near future.

It was a Friday (the Muslim holy day) and there were many family groups walking around the ruins and picnicking on the grass under the shadow of olive trees. It was warm, as good as a decent summer day back home in Kent and the world was at peace.

We still had 'Saladin Castle' at Ajloun, to see on the way back to Amman: Qal'at ar-Rabad, built in the twelfth century, of white limestone, was clean and complete; the crusaders had never taken it, nor had they extended beyond the Jordan Valley again after their defeat by Salah ad-Din at Hattin. The castle was impressive, but the main event of the day was the great Roman city of Jarash or Gerasa, referred to as 'the Pompeii of the East.' I walked around it for about two hours, taking a lot of pictures, as the air got cooler and the light softened. It had all the normal things an ancient Greco-Roman city should: a columned main street, two theatres as well as temples to Zeus and Artemis. There were churches and a synagogue, grand arches and city gates, also a repaired hippodrome, where gladiatorial displays and chariot racing happens on regular occasions. I wished I could have seen that really and would have planned to if I'd known.

My onward flight was scheduled for that same night, so, once we got back to Amman, it was the end of an insightful five days, in a country well worth a visit.

Mohammed took me to the airport although he didn't have to: it wasn't part of the deal I'd made with his boss and Mohammed didn't own the car. I felt like we'd genuinely become friends and it was a little sad to be saying goodbye.

CHAPTER FIFTEEN:

Jebel Shams

Oman was something different. I found what I was looking for there – the real Arabia, how I thought it should be.

The stamp in my passport read: *Sultanate of Oman* and my hotel had four stars! Yes, it was expensive in the capital, but not overdeveloped at all; Muscat was still traditional, vibrant and interesting. The ragged, dirt-brown mountains came right down to the sea, and the city nestled on a thin coastal strip within two sweeping bays that touched the Indian Ocean. The buildings were both old and new, and from my hotel, a twenty minute walk took me out of the edge of town and to the feet of a range of bone-dry mountains, baked brittle and crumbling in the hot sun.

I took a taxi ride into the centre of town and on the way, passed a roundabout near one of the beaches, with an old wooden, ocean-going *dhow* set up on a platform in the centre. On reading the information plaque, it turned out that this was the *Sohar*, the meticulously researched replica of an early medieval vessel that Tim Severin had built in 1980. I'd read the book, *The Sinbad Voyage*, which describes how the ship was built by hand at Sur, using no nails, but nearly four hundred miles of coconut-husk rope. It was then sailed to Canton, China, via Ceylon and Sumatra and the voyage had taken seven months.

Old Muscat was closed off to traffic when I got down there – due to a visit by Queen Elizabeth II, which I had been totally unaware of. I couldn't get anywhere near the Royal Palace, but the residential streets were thronged with people in traditional dress, waving flags, banging on drums and dancing.

The costumes the women proudly displayed were made up of beautiful turquoise silks, they wore make-up and lots of jewellery; the men were dressed in white robes with pill-box hats and they were all having a great time. It was a sort of time-warp, back to the 1970s, before the world had got all fundamental. I could see some African influence in the clothing, and in the faces of many Omanis; this had, after all, once been the Sultanate of Oman and Zanzibar.

I learned that the two main Arabian tribes here are descendants of the *Azd* from Yemen and the *Adnam* from the Nejd. This land was once part of the Persian Empire, so there was that heritage too, along with the results of centuries of sea trade with India.

The royal visit was part of a world tour of old Commonwealth nations, to commemorate the Queen's Diamond Jubilee. Politics and the New World Order aside, I was surprised that there would be such a welcome in a place like this; but there they were, waving the Union Flag alongside their own national banner, all smiles for my camera and that tongue warbling thing the women do.

I didn't see one glimpse of the darkness and resentment we've come to expect in these times, not a hint of it anywhere. There was none of that ethno-centric arrogance that rich Arabs are known for either. Oman is a traditional Islamic country, with a lot of wealth, however none of the new buildings I saw were taller than the mosques within the same communities.

During the few days that I spent in the country, I encountered no disdainful looks; there was no shouting, no hassle and none of that contrived overfriendliness. I found it expensive because of the exchange rate, but that didn't mean there wasn't a full radius of socio-economic layers, just as there should be in any naturally developed society. The Gulf States, on the other hand, are not natural and that's probably why they don't feel right; without oil to fuel investment, they would still be fishing villages, and probably a lot more friendly. Long before oil changed this region overnight, Oman had its own industries – accepted, one of them was the East African slave trade, but gold had always been traded for other luxuries here: frankincense for one.

In the south of the country is a region called the Dhofar, where an atmospheric phenomenon still forms mist on the coastal side of the uplands, and it is a verdant green during the *khareef* (monsoon), from July to September. There are birds and animals in these hills, and trees grow there; it is not by chance that this land is where the Queen of Sheba hailed from, and that the lost city of Uban (Atlantis of the Sands) lies buried somewhere beyond those southern hills.

The celebrations at the palace were still going on the next day and they were combining it with the commemoration of forty years in power for Sultan Qaboos Bin Said al-Said. I sat it out in my suburb on the edge of the city and that evening I went to an outdoor *shawarma* restaurant nearby, called *The Golden Sheep*. It was a busy place with the locals, simple, cheap food and no-one spoke English. I had no idea what things were called or what the dishes cost, but I trusted them there, and was treated well, just like any other customer.

There was a big TV mounted outside where we all sat and it was showing incredible displays of horsemanship in the grounds of the Royal Palace, for the entertainment of the Sultan and the Queen. I'd never seen anything like it; seeing riders standing astride three galloping horses was incredible enough, but a performance by one brave young man dressed in swirling silks and with a mane of black hair, like his own horse's tail, beggared belief. To crown his personal display at the end of it all, he swung underneath the belly of his galloping racehorse first, then climbed back round onto the saddle again, with the horse going full tilt towards the royal pedestal.

To close down the celebrations, the Sultan's honour guard stood in front of the British Queen and sang *Rule Britannia*, in Arabic – now that wouldn't even happen in London! Arabs and Indians sat there, riveted to the screen and it was glorious.

A few years before this trip, I had come across Ranulph Fiennes' brilliant autobiography: *Living Dangerously*. Although it covered a long list of inadvisably incredible journeys – and attempts to throw privilege to the wind and live life as one big calculated risk – what had mostly inspired me was his account of two years spent as a volunteer officer, seconded into the Sultan's rag-tag army. This opportunity had come about in 1966, as a result of getting himself expelled from the SAS at a time when the regiment was still a little-known-about association of reckless bravados. Incidentally, Fiennes beat the regiment to Oman by three years, as only in 1971 did SAS units get officially sent there.

My main fascination with the region, after having read that book, was not the military adventure concept, or the cult of personality, but the way the landscape and culture were directly connected and, in a way, this suggested that a bit of warfare, from time to time, was a natural human distraction from the hardship of the unforgiving climate and terrain. Whilst writing the initial rough manuscript for this work, sitting on my private balcony in Phnom Penh, Cambodia, I came across that same old book, amongst my collection there of old suitcases, stuffed with personal effects that had been stored there for many years – much of it the remnants of a set of circumstances, which had tied me to that tropical anti-paradise during the 1990s.

It seemed right that I should re-read the section about Fiennes' time in Oman. The story brought me to that spot in the Dhofar, where he'd described sitting up in a cave, on ambush duties at Wadi Dut. It was described so well that I felt I was almost there, in that heavenly setting, watching bemusedly as the three '*Bedu*' girls bathed in mountain-spring pools, fringed with flowering shrubs where humming-birds darted and hovered. The scene became a little less Eden-like a bit further into the wait, as the author recounted that, curiously just one of the girls had remained at the pools, soon to be met by her dark-skinned lover. Once the deed was done and the young man gone, so the account reads: '*the girl lay still for a while then walked with languid steps to the pool. She washed her face but not her body and disappeared behind the rocks.*'

I booked a car and a driver to take me to the mountainous interior and the high plateau of Jebel Shams – the third highest point in the Arabian Peninsular and referred to as the 'Mountain of the Sun.' We left at 08.30 and the first part of the drive was to the town of Nizwa; it was a good taster for me to get a feel for how life was for the non-urban population. The road passed between the mountains, running along dry valleys and Fanja was the first place we came to. It was a wadi town, where all the flat land was divided into various date farms. There were ancient watch towers sited part-way up mountainsides, suggesting a time gone by, when passage to and from the interior was under the control of regional militias.

We passed the turn off for Bidbid and then, after an hour or so, made a stop at Birkat al-Manz, a small town just off the highway, built on the edge of the flat, date palm valley that rested immediately below the stony mountainside. I learned that the town owed its existence to a permanent year-round water supply, from a natural spring that ran through a series of *aflaaj*, which were open cement channels – aqueducts really – that were only a few feet wide. This gravity fed system was originally set up by the Persians, over 2000 years ago, and it's still flowing.

The water springs appear a short way up the side of the mountain and the original 'City of Clay,' which begins immediately the land raises up, still stands on the steep slope, extending up to that point. I climbed up through the crumbling, abandoned village built of mud, straw and gypsum, over roofing beams of quartered date palm trunks. It was similar to the mud-built town of Old Siwa, where I had been years before, deep in the Egyptian Sahara. The difference was that: here most of the rooms were very small and cramped, and despite how it looked from the valley floor, the dwellings were all single stories, with the flat roof of each lower room becoming an open veranda for the one above. The stone slabs of the two stairways marked out the form of the triangular settlement and the two inclining trails both led up to the top of the whole structure and ended at the watchtower.

The air was hot and dry and so was my throat, but I got a good view from up there. Judging by the small amounts of debris left in some of the buildings, which included broken pottery shards and parched scraps of some pages from the Quran (Koran), I would estimate that the place had been unoccupied for something like forty years. That made sense, as it would have corresponded with the beginning of Qaboos' reign as Sultan and it was only after the Jebel wars that the oil money started seeping through to modernise the country. Even so, some of the houses at the foot of the abandoned village, that people certainly were living in, were made of clay construction too. Those newer houses were built to a comfortable size, though the only decoration I saw on some was the carving on the wooden doors.

Women gathered water from the *aflaaj* and donkeys carrying bundles of branches were led along the brown dirt road, past these simple but adequate homes. It was quiet there and didn't seem a bad place to be.

Nizwa was once the capital of Oman, I was told, and known as 'The Pearl of Islam' due to its status as a literary centre. It appeared, quite suddenly, at the confluence of two wadis. There was a castellated city wall and gates, which were well restored, and date palm gardens to give shade. Dominating the old town stands Nizwa Fort, with the souk close by. Despite the look of the yellow render, this was no sand castle, but a fortress to keep out any marauding army of tribesmen. The tower, which is nearly a hundred feet high and two thirds filled with earth and rubble, was built in the seventeenth century, as a base for cannon to fire out and over the city walls.

The Old Town itself was good for a walk around, with narrow streets as well as some old mud construction houses that were repaired and occupied. We stopped for some tea and my driver bought his lunch of small fried fish and shared some with me.

We drove on, up one of the wadis and into the hills on an increasingly narrow road. We passed Wadi Ghul, where a perfectly good stone-built village stands abandoned. Apparently the people re-located to a modern concrete village nearby; perhaps due to superstition, as the Arabic word *ghul* is the origin of our word ghoul.

Not far from that place the road climbed steeply and reduced to one lane; then we lost the tarmac completely as it became just a graded track. The modern Land Cruiser's gear lever was shuddering violently over the corrugations, but held the track well around the tight curves. We came out at Al-Hail, from where the military track went on up to the summit of Jebel Shams.

I found that the 'Mountain of the Sun' was without any specific summit – it was a cracked, rock-strewn plateau, dotted with stunted acacia bushes, roughly shield shaped where it had once been the sea bed. Way down, deep below the steep edge was Wadi Nakhr, a canyon five thousand feet deep, with a lace of pale green running through the centre: clearly a water source. I could see at least one small settlement, right deep in the bottom, where another spur of the canyon joined the main gorge.

About a mile ahead of me, and in a fan-shaped crack where the plateau tailed off down hill, was the *Bedu* village of Al-Khateem. I walked across to it, leaving the car and driver at the top of the track and I could see, as I got closer, that a trail led down and along from the village, into the steep canyon. The head of the canyon, nearby where the car was stopped, ends in a sheer cliff and although I saw someone walking along the trail that led towards the head, I couldn't see where this path could go to. Surely the people of Al-Khateem didn't have to bring water up from five thousand feet below – maybe they did?

When I got to the village on the highest plateau of the Hajar range – I found it to be more like a small farm, run by an extended family, than a real village. What I found was quite pitiful and entirely fitting to the circumstances: two old men in turbans, with beards and leather faces, were sitting under acacia trees, while some ragged and dusty children wandered about amongst the rocks and boulders, existing like goats and oblivious to the outside world.

Walking back up to the car was harder than it looked, due most probably to the altitude, and I couldn't help wondering what had put people on the top of a bare mountain in the first place. I realised that this was the first example I'd seen in Oman of any real poverty, which is quite a good point to any argument – certainly, on the whole, the Sultan has used his oil reserves to develop the country in a sympathetic way and I found it to be a polite and moderate Islamic society, which is way more than I can say about all the other Arab states that have built themselves up on the tide of the black gold.

CHAPTER SIXTEEN: Black gold

Seven or eight months after leaving Jordan, I'd taken the opportunity of a stop-over in the city of Kuwait. I had some expectations, due to the recent historical events there, but found the whole experience to be very unmemorable. It was not dissimilar to Qatar, but smaller and less well kept, which surprised me, and I wondered where all that regeneration money that was pumped into it after Gulf War One had gone to.

The place was positively shabby, in lots of ways. It was expensive and there was no culture to absorb. Asian migrant workers did everything and even the taxi driver I employed told me there was not much to see.

Kuwait is the name of a place everybody has heard of, but few people have chosen to visit. It was a gap in the map and so I wanted to have a look. The only thing I knew about it was oil wells and the Kuwait Towers, those strange bulbous spires out on a point by the sea – they were easily recognisable from all the news clips in 1991. When I got up to those iconic monuments they proved a bit of a disappointment too; they were much smaller than I'd imagined and not beautifully finished as I'd expected either.

My driver took me down along the coast road – really there was only one main road, other than the non-permitted routes that go out to the oilfields. The Maritime Museum seemed a possible diversion and it was; for less than half an hour. Attached to the museum was the most enormous and elaborate Arab dhow, recently built at the request of some rich oil sheik and dry-docked. It was all lavishly carved, and inscribed with gold decoration like a wooden palace. The museum proudly evidenced that the construction of this vessel had used up several hundred iroko and mahogany trunks harvested from the Congo, as well as other unrecorded amounts of sawn timber. It was certainly impressive, and the pictures showed how the ship was used to host classical music performances. I saw it as an enormous waste of the earth's recourses: a ship built, fit to sail the oceans, which had never been in the water and never will.

There was a man-made 'Green Island' that was slightly interesting to visit, with a sea-water lagoon inside its promenade; loud speakers were piping out recorded bird songs to create an impression of nature.

On the second day, I wanted to do a desert drive, but it quickly became clear that the desert was mostly just flat dirty plains, with some scrubby vegetation. I got my driver to take me out on the road that headed north to a coastal extremity I'd seen on the map. It turned out to be an old harbour spit with muddy bays either side of it and a low flat island. The peninsular of Doha Suburb, as it was called, was quite featureless but offered views of an oil fired power station on one side, as well as a dozen or more abandoned and derelict wooden fishing *dhows*, rotting in the mud just inside the spit. Those hulks had sat there, I thought by the state of them, since even before the war.

The National Museum was worth twenty minutes – there

really was so little there – as Kuwait didn't seem to have much of a history or a national identity. I have to say that the best of my experiences there was probably a visit to the Friday Market, on my second day in the city. It was a proper Arab souk, with all sorts of interesting junk for sale, as well as utilitarian stuff like quad bikes and fridges. There was no tourist tack as there were no tourists; I managed to buy an old tin dagger hilt and a real bride's cap there, very heavy to wear as it was stitched with strings of old coins.

To sum it all up: on my first morning out there I had enjoyed a walk along the beach front, where the sand was a pinkish-beige colour. I also enjoyed a small glass of sweet Egyptian-style tea; it was sold to me by an Arab with a proper tray full of glasses and a teapot, when I was in a little square near the main souk.

The Gulf States were becoming to me, at best an expensive diversion en-route to the Far East – however there was still Bahrain and Abu Dhabi to sample and I made sure I got to those places too.

Bahrain is an island, positioned between Qatar peninsular and the land of the Saudis. It is low, flat and relatively uninteresting. I did take some good pictures of the very fine-looking Qal'at al-Bahrain, which it turns out is a Portuguese fort, built around the much earlier archaeology of the site. It has a dry moat, cut into the surrounding wasteland that exposes the low-lying curtain-wall, which was obviously developed to be a defence against a seaborne enemy, as it is built just above the yellow sand beach. I found it a pretty sight, with the blue sea beyond it.

The island does have a couple of patches of natural mangrove forest, but really quite small areas – other than that, the only additional point of interest, if you don't care about lying on beaches with only one view, is the causeway bridge the Saudis have built. No one is allowed near it and it is only there to give access from the mainland. I was told that huge luxury vehicles are coming across all the time, as alcohol and cigarettes are readily available here. I was aware that there had been protests of some sorts, before I visited and then again soon after I'd left and I'd seen some political graffiti on buildings in one neighbourhood. I understood at the time that the unrest was connected with the King Fahd Causeway access; *Bahrain* has a Shi›ite Muslim majority and is ruled by a Sunni royal family. During the month following my visit, Saudi troops used that causeway and the Bahraini authorities declared martial law.

Looking back through my journals, I found that I'd written nothing about my short stay in Bahrain, as there was nothing really to write about.

Abu Dhabi, on the other hand, warrants a mention. Although it's a part of the UAE, and so not markedly different from Dubai, it has a spirit of its own; the fact that the city is built around various bays and a chain of islands, makes it quite interesting and attractive. This is a big money place, a millionaires' playground, but affordable for two or three days, as long as you don't need to have any fun yourself.

I couldn't find anything traditional about the city itself, and I didn't go inland, but there are mangrove tracts in a couple of places and a very impressive and quite beautiful 'Grand Mosque' that is a big tourist attraction – everything is new and everything is an attraction. You can visit the F1 Ferrari experience centre and, if you have the dollars to spare, even take one out on their private race track.

I took a bus out across the horseshoe bay to the public sand-strip and had an ice cream. From the light-house on the end of the spit, there is a great view of the high-rise buildings that cram into the down-town area; they shimmer in the haze and reflect off the still water in the bay. After walking myself back around the bay, I found that I couldn't locate my hotel.

All night-time entertainment goes on inside the licensed hotels where, if you are a foreign visitor, you can buy an alcoholic drink for about three times what it costs in Europe. My hotel advertised that it had three nightclubs and a bar. I couldn't afford to buy a drink in each one but I had a look. The 'Arabic Night Club' was just banks of tables and chairs, all facing a stage where two or three women swayed around a bit (covered from wrist to ankle) for the attention of a handful of Arabs who were sat alone, spaced out at various tables. The deal, as I could see, was that a customer would occasionally call a male door attendant over and ask him to present the girl he was appreciating with a small flower, which went on his bill. She didn't get off the stage to thank him until she had collected a bunch of them, and by then I'd finished my drink and I don't know what was supposed to happen.

The 'Indian Night Club' used more women for its Bollywood type performance on the stage, but very few customers sat at the tables lined in front and I didn't bother hanging about.

Now the 'Russian Night Club' was almost worth the cost of the entrance drink. It was still the same layout, but the Russian girls were hot, and they actually knew how to smile.

I ended my one short evening of entertainment at the hotel's piano bar; it was quite a good atmosphere really, with a live, European-style singer, a regular drinks bar with stools, and an international clientele – mostly European expats and African prostitutes. But there were expat women there too, and it was a no-hustle joint, not even a dive really – just people winding down after a days' work…or just starting their night's shift.

CHAPTER SEVENTEEN: Alpha and Omega

Thirty years and more have gone by since I first set foot on that exotic and exciting Promised Land – it is at least that to more than one group that would call it sacred or holy. The prophet Nostradamus referred to the Jews as 'The People of the Book' – 'the cruel sect of the Muslims' was his expression for those who would call all Christians 'the infidel' and many of the acts of our crusaders were certainly deserving of an ungodly title.

It is often thrown out as an accusation, that the Christian nations align themselves with Israel and are against anything Islamic: well, if there is some truth in this, then it has little to do with religious conviction on the side of the western powers. I wasn't expecting to be drawn into a discussion along these lines, when, a few years ago, I was taking in the evening air and all the sensations of a new and strange place like Bandar Seri Begawan; the tiny capital city, carved out of the Borneo jungle state that is the Sultanate of Brunei – it gets very little through traffic.

I had happened across a wide and pleasant pathway that led me away from the main crocodile river-front and into the main centre of town; it followed on an almost direct line with the glorious red sunset I was admiring. So I took this way and soon found myself looking at the silhouette of the City

Mosque. It had become quite dark, surprisingly quickly and I tallied a while, becoming interested by the symbolism of the robed figures entering and leaving the mosque enclosure. It was a little surreal, as I wouldn't normally associate the depths of a tropical jungle with the Arabian culture. I was there only a few minutes and a very respectable, well-spoken man greeted me as he came out of the gateway. I was there alone and happy to talk with someone and pass a bit of time. I don't remember his name, but he was tall with very dark African features and he told me he was from the UK.

I showed interest as a fellow British national, but also some curiosity, which my new friend picked up on. After a very short while of exchanging polite conversation, I knew I was being groomed. I told him that I was a Christian, or at least that I had grown up within a Christian culture and he talked about Christ being revered as an important prophet, but not the Messiah. It would all become clear, he said, 'when the Christians return to the right way, and we will be brothers again.' I questioned this, as I wasn't sure if it was some prophesy or just his statement of opinion. He was adamant: 'But we must kill the Jews first.'

'Why is that?' I asked. 'Isn't the Old Testament Bible the basis for all our religions? I know you have the Koran and we have the New Testament in addition, but why would we need to kill them?'

'Because they spread confusion' was the reply, and that was the only argument he offered me. I thought it might not be wise to offer an opinion there, as it would be based on my experience amongst the Jews, whilst working for the harmony of the State of Israel.

Brunei had not been my only association with Islam in the Far East. While travelling the length of the Indonesian archipelago in 1996, and on reaching the capital city of Jakarta on the main Island of Java, I did visit the old town called Kota, which was Dutch Batavia and the working port of Sunda Kelapa. This following account is how I wrote about the couple of days I spent in Jakarta:

The port was full of the traditional Makassar sailing schooners. They were loading and off-loading goods, some were having their wooden hulls repainted. There were fortified spice houses, the old Dutch watchtower and some rusted canons: the remnants of a great trading empire; crumbling walls holding back the refuse that was rotting in the stagnant channel below. There were market stalls and the narrow slum streets across the water. The grey open sewers and small canals, crossed by rickety wooden planks, were the veins of daily life, with small boats bringing goods inland from the port with the rise of the tide, which then took the sewage back out with it.

I got to witness a freak show in the street, amongst the rubble and filth; a group of amateur entertainers were playing drums and glockenspiels, as a fire eater, with sensitive lips, cracked a whip over the body of another member of the troupe, who was trussed up like a chicken. They had two vagabond boys, rolling around in the dirt, dancing and gurning in cloth hoods and masks; they seemed to be entranced. The one with the harelip was ducking for bits of vegetable in a bucket of dirty water and then he ate a light bulb and washed it down with some of that water. The whole thing was grotesque.

I met a bunch of university students on the train back to Jalan

Jaksa who fired off the usual questions at me. They were okay and walked me back to my block, where we sat in a café and drank lemon juice. The one girl in the bunch, Santi, who I didn't like much at first – she was a bit too quick and clever, with her baseball cap and American dialect – gave me her phone number as they left. I called her and we met up the next morning. We went around together the whole day and it was nice, apart from the arguments about East Timor and Saddam Hussein. We ate at an international café round the corner from my hostel and I ordered Indonesian, while she ordered Western food; we were both disappointed.

I believe we made a connection during those two days and I have often thought about Santi, and how her life might be turning out. She'd wanted to break out from the traditionalist Islamic lifestyle she felt her family would trap her into. She wanted what she thought we in the western cultured lands had, she'd declared that an Islamic veil on a woman did not indicate that she was any more virtuous than the next woman – I remember her telling me: 'It is just a mask.'

We exchanged some letters over time, and I learned that, in fact, she did get to travel abroad quite a bit: working in the Gulf to start with, and then on a cruise liner where her most exciting destination was the northern Israeli city of Haifa.

I lost contact with Santi after the millennium time hailed in a new era and aerogramme letters became something the modern world has forgotten all about. The new communication networks are all social media; even e-mails aren't used anymore by most of our new world's people. So I typed in a few likely combinations of her name and up popped a photographic image of a woman in a black niqab. Yes, it was Santi alright and what I could see and read on her site made me quite sad.

I did toy with the thought of making contact, to find out what had happened to turn that mentally strong, forthright and modern young woman, back a thousand years, to embrace a fundamentalist dead end – I thought about it.

It seems like everything in the Middle East has always been there and could last forever – other than the rocks and sand, there's all the hate and the love too – and then there's the oil; well maybe that will run out one day. Just off the coast of Dubai a series of sandy islands were artificially created to roughly represent an image of the whole globe, fractured into a collection of the major countries. It could only make sense when seen by satellite, but I thought it was quite novel.

The islands were intended as the ultimate luxury possession. But 'The World' is sinking back into the sea apparently, the channels through this archipelago are silting up and only Greenland has actually been occupied – how ironic is that!

CONCLUSION

This book would not be complete without revisiting some of the people who helped to make those early adventures so great:

Regarding my original first trip and my first great international adventure, I have met few friends from those days. Alan from the *Aram* still lives in Northfleet, by Gravesend. We had kept in touch for the first few years after the kibbutz, then lost contact until 2015, reunited thanks to the internet and the ever increasing tendrils of social media. My old pal turned up at a bonfire party I put on at the farm for that midsummer. The years had not been as harsh to Al as I might have expected – given his liking for the ale. He was there by a huge fire again and that's what counted.

Both the Marcelos are alive and well in Brazil, as are Maria Teresa and Jé. Alfonso, as much as I can work it out, is holding down some ambassadorial role in Europe, promoting a multi-national company. His images on the internet indicate that he has been living quite well for a long time. Katia had returned to the kibbutz around about the millennium and stayed there for six or seven years, before resettling in her homeland of Chile, Claudia is still happily married in Colombia and Jatziri is the Directora de Comunicación at WWF México.

As for Del, he lives in a Kent village, neighbouring my own, and is a grounds keeper for a local manor house estate. We have never not been in contact, and since the kibbutz times we have shared many an adventure together: including attempting to deliver humanitarian aid to the besieged Muslim towns of Mostar and Sarajevo in 1994, during the Balkan War.

Back in 1992, Sharon was preparing for his military service in the IDF. He had been the keenest of his age group at the kibbutz and, he said, the only one who had volunteered for a frontline combat role. I remembered him saying that he couldn't wait to shoot an Arab – or words to that effect. So when I made contact with him in 2018, via social media, and discovered he was a family man, living in Sydney, Australia, I was intrigued. I wanted to know how it had really been for him, outside the safety net of the Ramot Menashe fence.

We met in Melbourne in February of 2019; it was the Chinese New Year period and this one was for the Year of the Pig.

We talked keenly about the days back then, and I learned that old Nehemiah, the jeweller, had recently passed away. Gabi is still there, but he is thin now. Yonite and Yossi are still there, along with Mirriam, Shlomo and the delectable 'Miss Swimming Pool.' Niva (from the kindergarten) and her husband (another Yossi) from the bicycle work-shop have never left, but Dror (who is now bald) married a volunteer girl and went to live in South Africa. Aviv married twice, and is now bringing up six children; he moved out of the kibbutz and has a job working with problem kids. Phil actually did marry his last girlfriend, Yael, and they are probably still in Israel somewhere. Jesus lives at one of the neighbouring settlements, but he still plays the saxophone at Ramot Menashe for cultural evenings they put on. He has lost that hippy look though, and all the hair and braids that went with it.

Sharon himself, it turned out, was medically retired from

the army after being hit with shrapnel that entered the turret of a tank he was in. He'd done three years service, mostly Gaza and Lebanon, before the incident, and returned to the kibbutz, where he met his future wife (a fresh new volunteer) at the Terminal Nightclub.

It was great to meet up after all that time, and yes, war had changed him to a degree. There were still two things I wanted to know – and so I just asked: 'Did you get to shoot anyone?'

'Actually, yes I did.' Sharon answered. The Israeli accent had softened a bit but it was still there, and after two decades down under, I didn't really detect an adopted Aussie twang at all.

'And did he deserve it?' I asked.

'Oh yes…' came the reply and I believed it. Life expectancy of an Israeli soldier walking through Gaza unsupported, Sharon said, was fifteen to twenty minutes. That was where he said he was first taken on patrol with all the new recruits, to be goaded and pelted with stones, while ordered not to react. In the narrow streets they had to be aware of things being dropped from roof tops, like concrete blocks and fridges, but they were still not allowed to shoot.

After basic training, he had been sent to Lebanon; that's a place I've been interested in for such a long time and as I do like to have a joke, I asked if there were any coffee shops he could recommend to me: 'Sorry' he said, 'but my tank didn't fit in none of them' and we both laughed. As far as fear and anxiety were concerned, there'd been one particular situation my friend described, where he had really felt it. After receiving a call from another patrol, coming under fire at an undermanned outpost, Sharon's unit had to bring their tank along a road they were sure had been planted with at least one mine and they didn't know how far along the road would be safe, but they still had to make way. They'd covered half the distance, before receiving the call to stand down and turn back around. That kind of fear comes without the heat of battle rage and so it's often harder to handle; however Sharon said that, for most of the time in the southern buffer zone, it was boredom they had to contend with.

I hadn't known that Sharon's father was a holocaust survivor, originally from Budapest, although I remembered that there had been older people at the kibbutz, who still had their concentration camp numbers tattooed on their forearms. I didn't know his family when I lived there, but Sharon was a child of the Yom Kippur War. In 1973 his father had been in Sinai, fighting Egyptian forces (as had Nehemiah, who had been seriously wounded), when his unit was sent north to the Golan Heights to tackle the Syrians. He had stopped off at Ramot Menashe for one night, to visit his wife while he could and Sharon was born nine months later.

I found out that Sharon had been to Sinai for beach holidays at Dahab and Sharm el-Sheik, as have many Israelis since the peace treaty – he has no desire to experience the other Arab lands in the region, even though Jordan and Israel are now at peace and it would be an easy thing to do. It must rub a bit that when he holidayed in Malaysia with his Australian wife, he had to use his own Australian passport because Israeli citizens are banned from entering that most moderate of Islamic countries.

I noticed that he was wearing a Star of David pendant and when we went to eat at the best Chinese restaurant in Melbourne and the receptionist asked where he was from, the answer was 'New South Wales.' No other explanation. Being an Israeli in a world the rest of us mostly take for granted, is not the same as being a Scotsman in Yugoslavia, I suppose.

We talked about a lot of things, not just our past experiences. On my journey into the city I had seen two middle-aged, middle-class responsible-looking family men sitting at the top of the steps of some big official building in one of the main precincts. The large banner they sat either side of had read: 'FREE PALESTINE, BOYCOT ISRAEL' and I wondered how that made Jewish people feel, when they saw that sort of stuff. This has become quite a fashionably adopted band-wagon to sit on, for a lot of people with no connection to the Middle East, but who do cherish Western liberal ideals, it's a subject that can very easily start an argument no one's going to win. Sharon clearly wasted no time distressing himself over this kind of thing, dismissing it all as naïvely staged propaganda.

Back out on the street, as we walked beside the river, along the pedestrian precinct full of tourists admiring the Chinese New Year festive atmosphere, I asked: 'Do you still hate them?' I couldn't see how he wouldn't.

'It is not really hate' he said, 'It is defending against people who want to kill you.' We had got to where the precinct stopped, at one of the bridges linking the busy river banks and there were the rows of stainless steel bollards, cleverly designed to blend in. But they hadn't been there before the Islamic terrorists had recently started ploughing into people on busy city pavements, with cars and vans as the weapons of their perceived *jihad*. I could see how the four fins, or vanes that each bollard sported as if for ornamentation, would help to grip the smashed bodywork of a vehicle and help to prevent it from spinning out into the street. Without the internet, this new fear and hate couldn't have spread so quickly around the globe, and without the good intentions of nations of innocent people, it would never have got a foothold in our societies.

Sharon had laughed when I said that I knew the kibbutz volunteers had been third class citizens in those communities and I wanted to know what the *kibbutzniks* had really thought of us lot. 'We liked the volunteers' he said, 'especially the girls.' Well I knew that bit already; apparently there had been a couple of years in the mid-nineties when the kibbutz had not taken in any volunteers and we had been genuinely missed. I learned that someone had graffiti-sprayed a wall just inside the entrance gate during that time, with these words in Hebrew: '*BRING BACK THE VOLUNTEERS*' and this has been framed and preserved where it is, as a piece of the settlement's history.

An interesting snippet of information I gleaned is that Gabi used to share the application pictures of all the new girls, who were due to arrive, with the young lads who worked in the various stations and there would be some lust-fuelled discussions amongst them to decide how to share out the good-looking ones. We hadn't known that; most of the work places were mixed-sexes, but some were male or female oriented. So if you got the laundry or the kindergarten – that's because you weren't pretty enough to be chosen to work with the sheep. I think the boys just got put anywhere as an afterthought.

Anyway, those days are long gone and the kibbutz system is not that kind of commune society anymore. At Ramot Menashe the ghetto is history, as well as the basic student accommodation blocks. Terminal has been closed for many years, and even the dining room is not used as such anymore; it is used, but as a private outlet by just one family making and selling pizzas.

Now there is a highway viaduct passing right through the valley of the jackals, close to where the bee hive house was. There are no more avocados on the slopes and the people engage in private enterprise only. I had wanted to return one day and see the old place, but that era has passed and my memories are what I have left. It's good though, to know that we also made impressions that have not been lost in time.

THE END

BIBLIOGRAPHY

The Jerusalem Post (1989)

Dreaming of Jupiter, Ted Simon. Sphere (2007)

Living Dangerously, Sir Ranulph Fiennes. Atheneum Books (1988)

The Sinbad Voyage, Tim Severin. Hutchenson & Co (Publishers) Ltd (1982)

ACKNOWLEDGMENTS

Final acknowledgment must go to my big sister Lyn Taylor, for her much valued advice and editorial assistance, as well as her constant encouragement in all manors of pre-publication work, for which I am very grateful.

Jim Taylor